DATE DUE

LITERARY FRONTIERS

Also by J. DONALD ADAMS

THE SHAPE OF BOOKS TO COME

Edited by J. *Donald Adams*

THE TREASURE CHEST

Literary Frontiers

by

J. DONALD ADAMS

DUELL, SLOAN AND PEARCE
New York

KRAUS REPRINT CO.
New York
1969

Reprinted with the permission of the Licensor
KRAUS REPRINT CO.
A U.S. Division of Kraus-Thomson Organization Limited

All life remains unwritten still.—Emerson

CONTENTS

FOREWORD

This foreword is written at the end of a year which is not only the end of half a century, but the threshold of another which must prove to be one of the great turning points in human history. It is understandable, under these circumstances, that I should find myself thinking about books in long-range terms. They are, in their finest essence, men's hearts' blood. If they are literature in the best sense of the word, they speak to us all, regardless of sex, of class, of nationality. This capacity they have is endangered today as never before, as the shadow of the totalitarian state, carrying death to freedom of expression, lengthens across the world.

Even among ourselves, members of the free world, fundamental literary values have been obscured and lost sight of, time and again. Much of our writing about books fumbles about in a fog of conflicting ideologies. The practical problems, political, social, and economic, of our age press upon us with such urgency that we forget, in our preoccupation with them, that men everywhere, now

9

and always, meet the essential issues of human existence upon the same terms. Rich or poor, privileged or under-privileged, sophisticated or naive, intellectual or instinc-tual, life draws no lines where the basic human needs are concerned—the needs for love, for self-respect, for aspira-tion, for a life sustained by some meaning and purpose.

Literature is not a branch of sociology or economics, as some of our writers seem to suppose, or a branch of any-thing else. It is one of the great means that man has found of expressing his experience, whether it is the poet, pri-marily concerned with the individual's relation to life, or the novelist, whose interest is centered upon the individu-al's relation to his fellows. Literature means most to us, and is remembered beyond its immediate day, when it throws some light on what I have just referred to as the essential issues of human existence.

These are changeless, and until now they have con-tinued without regard to the form of government under which men live, influenced only in passing, and super-ficially, by the doctrines to which they subscribe at any particular moment. It is hard for us to realize this today, when, in the tense battle between conflicting ideologies, we feel that civilization itself, as we have known it, is threatened. But underneath, covered over by our con-temporary concerns, the essential issues are there.

The binding thread for the essays in this book is a sim-ple one. I have tried, as consistently as possible, to talk about literature in relation to life. The title derives from my belief that in our contemporary writing there are great unexplored areas. Some of them have been partially opened up, but much remains to be done. Only a part of this book is concerned with them, but I hope that there, as well as in the topics unrelated to that theme, the basic attitude of which I have just spoken has been maintained.

The greater part of what is contained here appeared originally in the weekly column, "Speaking of Books," in *The New York Times Book Review.* I have woven together, and in some instances, expanded, certain of these articles which were related to a common theme. I have included also a few pieces without direct bearing on the main topics of discussion. Certain passages in the book were first printed in articles which appeared in *The American Mercury* and *The Freeman,* and to these publications, as well as to *The New York Times,* I gratefully acknowledge permission to use material which they published. My thanks are due also to E. P. Dutton and Company for the use, in part, of the introductions I wrote for the American editions of the word anthologies of Ivor Brown.

J. D. A.

New York City, December 29, 1950.

LITERARY FRONTIERS

LITERARY FRONTIERS

Not long ago I spent a day sitting through a session of the United Nations General Assembly out at Flushing Meadows. In conversation with some of the delegates at luncheon I found myself drawing certain analogies between political and literary international assemblies, and I began to wonder why novelists have not made better and more frequent use of the richly suggestive material that lies in the altered behavior of men whenever they meet in large numbers, before an audience, to discuss matters of great or small importance. For in such circumstances a curious transformation occurs; their impulsions and motives are altered from the norm of everyday behavior, when their actions affect and are observed by only that small group of persons who know them well or whom they casually encounter.

It seems to be a kind of natural law of human conduct which dictates that the intellectual and ethical level ordinarily reached by individuals of even outstanding ability and character should automatically be lowered in proportion to the size of the group in which they function, and the degree of public attention which their acts command. In the course of my conversation with Dr. William Borberg, Denmark's scholarly and thoughtful delegate, we agreed that the prime factor in this scaling down of individual intelligence and principle to a lower group level is, obviously, the product of ego-satisfaction. I remarked that I had seen this same natural law at work in the international literary congresses of the P.E.N.; Dr. Borberg thought it was less evident in scientific assemblies and, partly for that reason, he believes that the interests of world peace might be furthered by an infusion of the scientific spirit in national and international political gatherings.

By this he did not mean government by scientific fiat, which might be as disastrous to human welfare as Shelley's conception, were it actual, of poets as "the unacknowledged legislators of the world"; but simply the acquisition of the scientist's disciplined determination to *know* before expressing an opinion, plus something of his dedication to truth. We were agreed, too, that better decisions might sometimes be reached if men worried at them less by rational processes, and could leave time for the powerful and often sure currents of the unconscious mind to assert themselves. Emerson, in other words, was not talking complete nonsense when he wrote about waiting for the oracle in the pine woods to speak.

It has since occurred to me that we might with profit

16

have discussed that engaging custom of the ancient Egyptians, as reported by Herodotus (whose eye for the interesting and significant detail our modern historians may regard with envy), of deliberating upon affairs of weight when they were drunk. On the following day, when they were sober, he tells us, the decision to which they came the night before was put to them by the master of the house in which it was made. If it was then approved of, they acted on it; and if not, they set it aside. Sometimes, however, they reversed this procedure; sober at their first deliberation, they would reconsider the matter with the aid of Bacchus.

To my thinking, this practice makes it more than ever plain that the Egyptians were a people of superior intelligence, in whose way of life we might find a profitable hint or two for our guidance. In its balanced approach to the process of arriving at judgments tinctured with wisdom, the custom of which Herodotus informs us seems to me nothing less than a stroke of genius. It insures boldness tempered with caution, and unfettered imagination checked by the tight rein of common sense. Why the entire world has not adopted it as standard procedure in all our courts and deliberative assemblies is beyond my comprehension.

Be that as it may, there are obviously themes and motivations peculiar to the phenomena which Dr. Bomberg and I discussed, which contemporary novelists, in their efforts to come to grips with the issues which occupy men's minds in this crucial century, have only lightly brushed, where they have paid any attention to them at all. I can, as a matter of fact, think of but one contemporary novel, Howard Spring's *Fame Is the Spur*, in which awareness of man's dual nature as expressed in his separate political and his more narrowly social selves, is interestingly explored. Our fiction, when it has occupied itself with that inner life of man which must be the serious novelist's deepest concern, has for the most part tended to restrict itself to individual conflicts, repressions, and complexes divorced, in the novelist's consideration of them, from their impinging effects upon other people, and upon the well-being of society as a whole. Our psychologically minded novelists have been content to explore merely their own egos; their preoccupations have been basically adolescent, whether they write with a pseudo-objectivity, like Hemingway, or with an unabashed absorption in their own growing pains, like a multitude of autobiographical novelists who demand that you, the reader, be the witness of their struggle out of adolescence into something resembling maturity. Say what you will about the Victorians, they got outside themselves and under the hides of their characters to a degree which the novelists of our own period seldom achieve. They had not become so involved in the contemplation of their own personalities as to be shut off from understanding of and sympathy with the people of whom they wrote. While it would be nonsense to pretend that any novelist writes completely without projection of himself into the men and women of whom his story is told, the effort to achieve this detachment is one in which American novelists particularly, I think, have fallen far short.

Why, I wonder, even when the habit of self-analysis was less commonly a characteristic of American writers, have our novelists shown so little inclination to depict the interesting sea-change which occurs whenever the individual becomes conscious of the reaction to his words and acts, not only of those with whom he works, but of the spectators as well? The neglect of this fascinating area of human conduct seems all the more surprising in view of our belief that we are a politically minded people. Actually, of course, as more than one foreign observer has pointed out, our national interest in politics—aside from those men and women whose profession it is—is a superficial and spasmodic one rather than a steady object of study. For the great majority of citizens it becomes engrossing only at four-year intervals, and even at these peaks there are not infrequent occasions (a close race in the World Series, let us say), when campaigns are conducted in an atmosphere of lassitude or indifference. Matters have indeed come to the pass where it takes an issue that strikes at some deeply imbedded part of the American credo—like the attempted "packing" of the Supreme Court—to arouse what has become a normally lethargic electorate. This is not the place to inquire into the whys and wherefores of the growing shallowness of

American political emotions and convictions, at least in the field of domestic issues; suffice it to remind ourselves of the days when the atmosphere round the cracker barrel was charged with thunder and lightning readily released. I say this much only because of its possible bearing on our novelists' choice of material. The kind of theme of which I have been speaking requires more than superficial handling, but even on the level at which politics have been treated in the American novel, the record yields a surprisingly small number of books in which the politician, let alone the statesman, has been subjected to anything more than cursory scrutiny.

If you look into the matter, you will find that by far the largest group of novels dealing with the political arena falls into the period of the muckrakers, when our magazine article writers were busily occupied in exposing corruption in local politics. Thus you find, in 1902, Brand Whitlock's *The 13th District*, and a year later, Alfred Henry Lewis's *The Boss*; in 1905 there was Booth Tarkington's *In the Arena*, and in 1906 Winston Churchill's (remember when he was even better known to us than his British namesake?) *Coniston*, which had for its subject the rise to power of a local political boss.

At the risk of wrecking the reader's train of thought—and my own—I interject here some mention of the delightful interchange of letters which took place in 1899 between the two Winstons. They are published in the more illustrious Churchill's account of his early life, issued in the United States under the title, *A Roving Commission*. He remarks that in the spring of 1899 he became conscious of the fact that there actually was another Winston Churchill who wrote novels for which his British namesake frequently received congratulations. (It is not surprising, in view of the former P.M.'s remarkable versatility, that he once wrote a novel entitled *Savrola*, which was written in two months, and yielded a profit to its young author of seven hundred pounds.)

In his letter to the American Winston, Churchill announced his intention of signing all future work "Winston Spencer Churchill" and suggested that each Winston insert an explanatory note in his future published works. The American novelist expressed appreciation of the other's courtesy, agreed to the suggested cooperation, and remarked that he was considering the insertion of the words "the American" on the title pages of his books.

Prior to the flock of novels dealing with local politics which I have just mentioned, there had been little worth noting, save Henry Adams's *Democracy*, anonymously published in 1880—one of our amazingly few novels dealing with life in the nation's capital; it was a story of social and political intrigue in which President Hayes was introduced under another name. There was also Paul Leicester Ford's *The Honorable Peter Sterling* (1894), which, in slightly disguised form, recounted the early political career of Grover Cleveland, and Ellen Glasgow's *The Voice of the People*, which dealt with the rise to Virginia's governorship of a back-country boy. Still earlier there had been, of course, the story which Mark Twain wrote in collaboration with Charles Dudley Warner under the title, *The Gilded Age.*

No American novelist has written a series of political novels (unless you admit Upton Sinclair's Lanny Budd series to that category), as did Benjamin Disraeli. But the British record is rather scanty also; there was Bulwer Lytton, to be sure, and Trollope, though Trollope's politicians did not assume the dimensions of his clergymen. Balzac, of course, did not omit the politician from his marvelously comprehensive picture of the Paris and France of his time; he is too much an integral part of the spectacle to which Balzac addressed himself in the panels of his *Comédie Humaine.*

I have been thinking, too, of other areas of our national life which have been skimped in our fiction. New Yorkers, of whom I am one born and bred, don't, I have long been convinced, unless they have been early and frequently exposed to other environments, really know what life is all about. Neither, I suspect, do Bostonians, Philadelphians, or Chicagoans, and most certainly not Angelenos (as I believe the citizens of that monstrous blot on the American landscape occasionally refer to themselves). I am talking primarily, of course, about those who were born and brought up in any of these great cities, unless they were reared in one of those self-contained little neighborhoods which still persist in some of our metropolises; and even there, they are part of a much larger community whose members are insulated against life as the inhabitants of a small town or village are not. Those who come to the great cities from the towns and villages (and from their ranks most of our novelists are drawn) have had a better education in humanity; but even they have failed to give us the same sort of inclusive picture of big-city life that Balzac created from his Paris.

Recently I read an obituary published on the front page of *The Vineyard Gazette*, regarded by some perhaps prejudiced observers as the best weekly newspaper in the United States. It announced the death of the oldest resident of Martha's Vineyard, Theodore S. Wimpenney of Edgartown, who, had he lived a few months longer, would have rounded out a full century of life. Many of the facts of that life are of interest only to his fellow islanders—the four-year whaling voyage on which he embarked at the age of seventeen, his later work as a carpenter, and his long years of service as a court crier. But Vineyarders or not, all readers can enjoy the fact that on his ninety-eighth birthday, which he had to spend in bed, he flexed his right forearm and said, "I believe

I could still strike a pretty powerful blow!" One likes to learn, too, that at the age of sixteen "he could earn the wages of a man because he could do a man's work."

The story of his funeral, as carried in the *Gazette's* next issue, began by recording the fact that the bell of the Congregational Church in Edgartown slowly tolled ninety-nine times, once for each year of his age. His former pastor, who spoke the words of tribute, had this, among other things, to say about him: "He had in him something of the straightness and simplicity of the age whose spirit built fine clean houses like this old church in which we gather to remember him. He had something of the staunchness and fundamental honesty of the ships in which he and his fathers sailed and of the houses which his workman's good hand builded. New times have come and we are too busy to seek for the right simplicity, but we pray that enough of his kind of heritage has entered into us to hold us if 'the hurricane comes.'"

From this kind of community experience the big-city resident is too often cut off. The obituaries which he reads in his morning paper are too often the stories of lives which have never touched his own. What was it that gave such poignancy to William Allen White's famous account of his daughter Mary's death, aside from the fine simplicity of the writing, if not the fact that this was a tragedy in which an entire community closely shared? Mary on the horse who carried her up to the tree limb that dashed her from the saddle was to all of them a long-familiar sight, and her cheery greeting a well-remembered part of any day. What was it that made the pitiful story I read in my New York paper the other morning, about the poor child who took her life because the boy she was expecting did not call, moving only as something that we read in a book may move us? Only to her family's neighbors did it come truly home.

Perhaps we have here the reason why so few native New Yorkers have been able to write with truth and feeling about the city of their birth. Henry James's New York was the New York of the great world; so too was Edith Wharton's. Who are the New Yorkers born who have made their city live in fiction? Can we name one who has caught and held in his pages the myriad facets of its life, in whose work we find reflected not only the teeming tenements of the lower East Side, or the roaring Forties, but also the placid Brooklyn streets, the huge steel-and-stone packing cases of Park Avenue, the crush and loneliness of the subway, the Central Park of the lovers, the bird-watchers, and the hoodlums? A bit here and there by this man and that; that is all.

We fare a little better when we think of O. Henry, who, say what you will about the contrivances he employed, and the blight he is accused of having laid on the American short story, did manage surprisingly well to catch the feeling and the atmosphere of the New York of his time. But he was a boy from Greensboro, North Carolina.

The most successful attempt at a kaleidoscopic picture of New York in fiction was Dos Passos's *Manhattan Transfer*, but he was born in Chicago and spent a good part of his childhood abroad. Even the best non-fiction piece about New York—E. B. White's fine portrait— was written by a man who was born in Mount Vernon at a time when residents of that suburb could, after not too long a walk, come to woods where the chestnuts could be shaken down. Thomas Wolfe must not go unmentioned, because he wrote pages about New York and its people which had great power. But what have we now, from the bright young men who come to town from Kansas and Iowa, from Oklahoma and the Carolinas, to work in publishers' offices, on newspapers and magazines, and in those graveyards of literary talent, the advertising agencies? Stories about writers and publishers, about newspaper and magazine tycoons, about the big shots of the advertising world.

Now this is only natural; they reach out for their living points of contact with the city to which they have come, and now and then we get from these sources a vital novel like Mr. Wakeman's *The Hucksters* or a thoughtful one like Mr. Brooks's *The Big Wheel*. Like all great cities, New York is made up of many worlds, and it is not surprising that, if our young novelists are to write of New York at all, their concern should be with the particular world which they have known at close quarters. My impatience with the prevalence of this sort of fiction—aside from the fact that there is so much of it—has its roots, I suppose, in the fact that writers ordinarily make difficult material for other writers to write about in fictional form. Too much of their lives is lived inside themselves to make for easy narrative interest. It is a simple matter, of course, to name exceptions among those who are half men of action like Byron, but theirs is not the prevailing pattern, and less so, perhaps, in our time than in others. Editors are even less promising material than writers; publishers and advertising tycoons are likely to have a more extroverted air.

Those few novels about writers which the world has taken to its heart have not been overly concerned with their literary travail. One thinks of Thackeray's *Pendennis* and finds it hard to proceed further without recourse to the reference books. In our own time the book that comes first to mind is the delightfully satiric tale told by Somerset Maugham in *Cakes and Ale*. He managed to suggest that his Grand Old Man of English letters—not, he insists, to be confused with the actual figure of Thomas Hardy—while unquestionably a writer of considerable gifts, had as his outstanding claim upon our attention not so much the qualities intoned by the critics as the one conferred by his longevity.

A risky business, this, of trying to convince your readers that you are writing about a great writer—more so, perhaps, than if your protagonist is presented as a great singer, actor, musician, or painter, for it is much easier, in the case of these others, to convey the impression of greatness which they themselves conveyed, and how it was done. Charles Morgan tried it once, you may recall, in a novel called *Sparkenbroke,* and came a cropper.

In spite of my dislike of the surfeit of stories about journalistic and literary New York, it is one of my convictions that what matters least about an author's work is his choice of material. It seems like stating a too obvious truth—and I have stated it before—that what really matters is what he does with that material, what he brings back from that particular world of his observation and imagination he has entered, but I think it needs emphasis because in recent years we have seen too much value given and too much attention paid to his choice of material.

The prevalence of this attitude has given rise to a great deal of unjust and irrelevant criticism. Not only have fledgling writers suffered by it, but some of our most distinguished and accomplished craftsmen as well. This certainly was true of the ill-concealed or quite outspoken hostility with which the choice of themes in her later work was treated in the case of Willa Cather. It is an attitude which has been used as a stick with which to beat John Steinbeck. And chiefly, perhaps, it has been used as a blanket indictment of the historical novel, where its falsity and inconsequence is, perhaps, most readily apparent. A writer does not necessarily retreat from his own age or fail to bring illumination to it merely because he sets the time of his story at an earlier hour. Truth and light are not so time-bound as that. And our writing, as a matter of fact, is overweighted with contemporaneity.

Timeliness lies on our literature like a curse. But, you may say, is not this to be expected and even desirable when our problems are so pressing and so ubiquitous; how can you reasonably expect writers, in a time when the world is one great tinder-box, to keep enough serenity to give their work that quality of timelessness which sets the great books apart? The answer seems to me obvious: how are we to meet, even to face, these problems with courage and resolution and clear sight, unless we view them in the long perspective and with the balance that our preoccupation with the immediate cannot yield? Our insistence upon our day and hour reveals itself in its effect upon many fields of writing: here is John Gunther, one of our best reporters, rich in vitality and insatiable in curiosity (both valuable factors in his equipment), loading down his *Inside U.S.A.* with an interminable Who's Who of evanescent local politicians, in a book that might have penetrated to the essential qualities of our several regions, instead of piling up a list of facts, many of them fascinating, about the forty-eight states. Again the overmastering urge to be timely at all costs, which too often means to be unmindful of the slower and deeper currents that lie beneath the brisk eddies at the surface.

I suppose, as a matter of fact, that the travel book as

we have known it on its highest level, is doomed to extinction, and may not be expected to rise again unless our world is swept clean, and left for new interpreters to examine when its successor takes form. Restless movers about though we are, the travel book has not been our forte. We have contributed no monumental classic like Doughty's *Arabia Deserta* nor, on another rather less ambitious plane, a book as good as Tomlinson's *The Sea and the Jungle*. Our best books of the kind have been done on home ground: such books as Bartram's *Travels*, Catlin's *Eight Years*, and Parkman's *Oregon Trail*. The immortal writers of travel have been born elsewhere, more than a fair share of them, perhaps, in the British Isles. Heaven knows the British have added enormously to the number of mediocre and downright dull chronicles of the wandering foot—those lovingly compiled and boresomely detailed volumes which have whiled away the sunset hours of so many retired British colonels and civil servants—but they have also added more than a few to the permanent shelf.

The chances are weighted, it seems to me, that in the years immediately ahead we shall see very little travel writing of the enduring kind. Aside from the competition offered by the movies in a picture-conscious period, and the magic carpet woven by the airlines, there is the probability that if our world holds together at all, most books about other countries will be, as they have been for some time past, if not merely handbooks, primarily concerned with their social and political complexion at the precise moment of the writing. During the long years of reconstruction and reorientation which we face if the race survives, it seems more than likely that our writing about other countries will continue to be of that same nature. The old travel books were like a series of still pictures, however vivid and revealing. The rapidly shifting world we live in now, and which will be the lot of a generation or more to come, encourages nothing of the kind. Our recordings in print of countries overseas will be largely action pictures, momentarily catching the flux in which our whole world is enwrapped.

If our novels have dealt only superficially with the politician and fragmentarily with the life of our great cities, what are we to say of their handling of that most typical of all American figures since the 1870's—the businessman? One of his first full-length portraits was that drawn by William Dean Howells in *The Rise of Silas Lapham*, a book which we might choose as emblematical of the first stage of that treatment. In the second we might select Dreiser's Cowperwood series, and for the third, Lewis's *Babbitt*. Each performed a useful job: Howells, with balance and no small amount of sympathetic insight, studied that particularly American phenomenon, the self-made man; Dreiser, with single-minded ferocity, concentrated on his piratical aspect; while Lewis, in satire tinged with affection, approached him in his role as philistine. Since Howells, few American novelists have written of the businessman with objectivity; except for the unrealistic, formula-ridden stories of the popular magazines, he has consistently been pilloried in one way or another.

Granted even the abuses in American business and the predatory character of so many big business leaders during our period of great material expansion, an attitude of condescension and dogmatic antagonism has characterized the approach of the liberal intellectuals (if I may permit myself the use of two meaningless words) to that large segment of our national life centered in the man of business. In some respects that attitude has been basically and half-unconsciously, I think, a compensation for the disdain and contempt in which the writer and the artist were held by "practical-minded men" during the term of America's Gilded Age, reinforced by the age-old natural mistrust and lack of sympathy between the doer and the contemplative man.

As manifested in our fiction, the adoption of this attitude has had aspects which are both ridiculous and unfair. Since our beginnings as a nation, more than a proportionate share of our best brains, more than a majority, perhaps, of American men of first-rate capacity, have chosen to direct their energies into the fields of material effort. Their adoption of such careers has sometimes been fortuitous, sometimes the result of unwillingness to be content with the meager rewards offered by our society for comparable performance in the fields of intellectual and artistic effort. But your really first-rate man, your man of genius and great energy, has always been able to distinguish himself in various and quite unrelated fields. The elder Morgan, had he so chosen and willed, could no doubt have made himself as eminent a mathematician, astronomer, or physicist as he was a banker. Mr. Churchill, among our contemporaries, is an even more obvious example, living, as he does, two or three lives in one. We would know his name if he had never held political office.

A year or two ago, in *Fortune,* John Chamberlain wrote a brief survey of the American businessman in fiction, in which he amusingly re-created for the purposes of his article the figure of Booth Tarkington's Mr. Tinker, twenty years older than he was in *The Plutocrat,* one of the very few sympathetic novels about the businessman written since the first decade of this century. Through Mr. Tinker's eyes, Mr. Chamberlain asked us to observe the "Dance, tenderfoot, dance!" routine through which our novelists have put that chief object of their scorn, the American doer, whether he be Cowperwood, Babbitt, or Dodsworth in type. Mr. Tinker found it hard to understand why practically all businessmen portrayed in our recent fiction seemed to have been born with horns.

Mr. Chamberlain, like myself, was well aware that the writing of novels such as *The Titan, The Financier,*

Babbitt, or, more recently, such a book as Mr. Wakeman's *The Hucksters,* has been necessary and salutary for our literary and cultural development, but—and the "but" is a big one—if our latter-day novelists, he pointed out, had continued the tradition of what Vernon Parrington called "critical realism," if they had continued "putting corruption within a perspective that also includes the comparative honesty of most business people, there would be no cause for Mr. Tinker's complaints. But what gives Mr. Tinker's type of flareback its justification is that 'critical realism' has ceased to exist. The modern novelist is emotional and subjective when he approaches the theme of United States industry; he does not look at it in the light of changes that he himself has helped to instigate." He has paid little or no attention to the evolution of the American big business man. There is a great gap between the robber baron of the gilded age and the enlightened leader of contemporary industry.

When I broached this topic in *The New York Times* Mr. Max Lerner sprang to the defense of our young novelists: "What they are saying," he contended, "is not so much that the Big Business man is a stinker . . . as that they intend to have no traffic with concentrated monopoly power that is not responsible and responsive to the people. . . . They have glimpsed that power can be private as well as governmental, that democracy can be stifled by the greeds and fears of financial movers and shakers as well as by the power lust of commissars." That is all very well, but are they to take no cognizance of the existence of such a thing as enlightened big business and its forward-looking leaders? Is that part of our fiction which takes the American business scene for its province to be as stereotyped in its approach as the Russian novel written in the shadow of the Kremlin? One of the prime factors that made Russian fiction so powerful in its great period was its intense awareness of man's duality, a sense that has been largely lost in the decline of that "critical realism" of which Parrington spoke.

In what remains of this chapter I should like to touch upon one more area of American life which, it seems to me, has been insufficiently handled in our creative literature. Only within the last few years have our poets and novelists—our playwrights not yet at all—begun to come seriously to grips with that great fact of American history, the westward movement. Yet the effects of that experience upon us were profound and continuous; the advancing frontier that so long possessed our energies is still the key to the understanding of many facets of the American character.

We have a history now that covers three and a half centuries, and during much the greater part of that time it was the history of the land, in the words of Robert Frost's poem, *The Gift Outright*, "vaguely realizing westward." As much as a hundred years ago the pattern of that movement was set, the quality of its drama estab-

35

lished, and its poetry, as well as its economic fact, evident. Is it not strange that our poets did not more often, and more successfully, attempt this theme in an epic manner? What is there aside from John G. Neihardt's *The Song of Hugh Glass* and that projected work of Stephen Vincent Benét of which he was able to complete only the first volume, *Western Star*, before his untimely death?

And is it not strange that the Rocky Mountain West, so deeply American, so significant a part of our history, should have had to wait so long for anything like adequate treatment in our fiction? Out of its rich material there came for a long time only the most stereotyped kind of story—the Western that the movies are now spawning in such profusion—and employing only the most obvious and melodramatic facets of its character. Only in the last few years have writers like Conrad Richter, Walter Van Tilburg Clark, and A. B. Guthrie approached that material with a sense of its full potentialities.

As a matter of fact, the regional resources of American fiction—and among them some of the most potentially fruitful and interesting—have still to be adequately explored. The Southwest and the Northwest are practically untapped. Out of the first we have had but one first-rate novel—Willa Cather's *Death Comes for the Archbishop*, together with part of a less successful story of hers, *The Professor's House*. The high-water mark in fiction dealing with the Northwest was set by H. L. Davis, in *Honey in the Horn*, and that was more than a decade ago. Even the Deep South, which has been so much to the fore in the fiction of recent years, waits for a fuller interpretation. There are aspects of the South, other than those which Ellen Glasgow, William Faulkner, and Eudora Welty have set forth, which are still to be reflected in our novels; and no part of the country is changing more rapidly. The Middle West, which was for a time the focal center of American fiction, is due for a new phase in its literary history. Just as surely as the young Middle Western writers of the Twenties rebelled against their background and fled to the Left Bank, those of the Fifties are likely to identify themselves with the towns and the countryside from which they came. May not Ross Lockridge's *Raintree County*, confused though it was, have, in its feeling of attachment and its sense of identification, pointed to a turning of the tide?

But I have wandered a little from my chief concern at the moment, which is to ask why we have been so slow to develop in imaginative terms a comprehensive view and interpretation of our experience in the westward movement, so thoroughly and extensively examined by our historians. I have the feeling that our failure to do so explains something in our cultural composition that it might be well for us to understand. What makes the failure all the more puzzling is the fact that the theme is so obvious, and so central to the emotional and rational reactions of every American. The pioneer experience—either the actual participation in it, or the sense of it which we have gathered either from parents or grand-parents, or from our reading—has left a deeper impress on American life than anything else except two quite different influences which were brought to bear on us much later: the automobile and the movies. All three of them had their negative as well as their positive effects upon our development.

The positive effect of the first was never more succinctly stated than by Frederick Jackson Turner, in the concluding paragraph of that pioneer work in the interpretation of the role of the frontier—*The Frontier in American History*. "This, then," he wrote, "is the heritage of pioneer experience—a passionate belief that a democracy was possible which should leave the individual a part to play in free society and not make him a cog in a machine operated from above; which trusted in the common man, in his tolerance, his ability to adjust differences with good humor, and to work out an American type from the contributions of all nations—a type for which he would fight against those who challenged it in arms, and for which in time of war he would make sacrifices, even the temporary sacrifice of individual freedom and his life, lest that freedom be lost forever."

May it not be that the answer to my question lies in the word "movement"? Always, in the very nature of this national experience of ours, there was a tearing up of roots, and thus there was no crystallization of this experience for the artist to seize upon. For cultural dependence on the mother country, by which we were handicapped for at least two centuries of our existence, is not the only reason why creative literature develops slowly in new societies. There is also the factor that the material with which the artist must work is in a state of constant flux: types, attitudes, customs, whether of individuals or of groups, are only in process of being formed, thus making the task of the novelist, in particular, more difficult. The great novels of eighteenth- and nineteenth-century England, of nineteenth-century France and Russia, reflected societies which had acquired a definite, temporarily fixed character.

It was accordingly no accident that the first great American novel, *The Scarlet Letter*, was produced under somewhat similar circumstances. New England was the first section of the country to crystallize in character, and Hawthorne's novel had its roots deep in the material which is used. Its author was as intensely identified with the background of his work as were Fielding, Jane Austen, Balzac, Dickens, or Tolstoy. When I spoke a moment ago about the work that remains to be done in making creative use of regional material in certain parts of the United States, I was thinking, of course, of this kind of identification. It was Van Wyck Brooks who pointed out the difference between regional writing in the best sense and the mere use of "local color." He observed that the work of writers like Bret Harte was concerned with painting the elements of oddity and quaintness in the local scene, whereas the deeper regionalism for which we are now looking—and which we have begun to get—is not primarily concerned with these superficial differences. It rises out of the writer's oneness with his background, and his effort to understand and interpret it.

Regionalism is, if you like, a kind of crutch used by the novelist in his attempt to probe the significance of human lives, but it is one that some of the greatest writers have employed, and that has proved especially helpful to Americans. In a country as large as ours, with such deep-seated regional differences (in spite of all the to-do that has been made over standardization and the multiplication of Main Street), it was inevitable that it should bulk large in our writing. It is possible, too, as Mr. Brooks also suggested, that New York's failure to mirror the country as a whole, in the way that London and Paris have mirrored England and France, has exaggerated this natural tendency.

The regional writing that we will have during the years immediately ahead should probe more deeply and yield more fruitful results than much of the earlier spade-work. I think this likely because the generation from which this writing will come has seen more of the world than any recent American generation. It has bases for comparison, for judgment and understanding in which its predecessors, for several generations, had been lacking. Nor is that the only reason for such a hope. There has been for a good many years now a great outpour-

ing of books of a kind which often serves to set creative impulses in motion. I am thinking of all the writing we have had which has been lighting up the little
known or forgotten corners of American history, and all
the regional writing of a factual kind—the sort of thing
typified by the Rivers of America or the American Folk-
ways Series. Many of the books in these fields are crammed
with material that carries within it the seed of suggestion.
They have made us more conscious of many facets of
American life, both past and present. Even to those
native to a particular region, they have opened up fresh
vistas, new avenues of understanding. It is all very well
to say that literature is made from life, not from books,
and so, basically, it must be, if it is to have vitality, but
we have only to remember the transformations wrought
by Shakespeare in the printed material which came to his
hand, to realize how large a part books of the kind I
have mentioned can play in stimulating the creative
process. And so I think a lot of groundwork has been
and is being laid for the use of the westward movement
as a widely conceived, embracing theme.

In the essay that follows I turn to another unexplored
area in our creative writing—one which though it has
scarcely been touched, is far more important than any
I have mentioned. There are two great issues in our time:
one is the survival of a free society; because its pressures
are immediate and inescapable, it finds its way irresistibly
into our minds and into our books. The other, while no

less real, is much less immediate and much less definite. But it has, I am sure, an equally important bearing on the future. This issue revolves about the relations between men and women.

WOMEN AND FICTION

           I approach this topic with something like fear and trembling, because if there is anything an ordinary experience of life should teach, it is that the generalizations made by the members of one sex about those of the other are the most perilous of all. Nevertheless, there are some things I want very much to say about women as readers and women as writers, especially as viewed in relation to the changing status of women in our society. For it follows as the day the night that any change which is occurring among women must be of vital interest to men as well, or should be. That a really profound change has been going on, to a still undetermined outcome, every intelligent woman is today aware; most of them, I think, believe that men in sufficient numbers are not yet fully awake to it. And, I suspect, they are right in believing so.

My suspicion strengthened recently when a well-known popular writer observed in print that one of the fundamental decisions a writer must make today is whether he is going to write for men or for women. He was speaking with the conditions prevailing in the United States particularly in mind when he went on to say that "in one sense it's no decision at all; the decision is made for the writer. If he wants to earn a decent living, he must write for women."

Now it seems to me that if he had been thinking in terms of conditions obtaining in 1870, or even in 1900, he would have hit much nearer the truth. It is perfectly true that the number of magazines addressed primarily to women has greatly multiplied, and continues to do so; it is equally true that editors and book club judges are aware that the greater part of this country's reading is done by women. But the nub of the matter is not the size of this feminine audience, but the range of its interests. Surely there can be no doubt that the American woman of today, whether housewife or career woman, far outreaches her sister of 1870 or of 1900 in that respect. She may not be happier, or as happy; she may, even, at this acutely transitional stage, be less of a woman; but there can be no discounting the fact that her outlook has broadened immeasurably.

When the average American girl marries today, she has had at least a glimpse into that masculine world which was, for much the most part, a mysterious *terra incognita* to her Victorian predecessor. If, as often as not, she happens to have a lively intelligence, she is not too greatly impressed by the mysteries there revealed to her. And when she assumes, if she does, the role of housewife, she carries with her an idea or two concerning male pretensions which her grandmother would never have admitted to her consciousness, unless she happened to be one of the then infrequent rebels of her sex who insisted on doing her own thinking.

The American male writer, according to the lament raised by the representative I have mentioned, must reconcile himself to the fact that he is writing principally for women. So what? Actually, it seems to me, there never was a time in the history of the printed word when the writer had to give less thought to the question of whether he was addressing men or women. I think this to be true even if we narrow our consideration of the question to the reading of fiction, in which women, now as always, take the predominant part. Women, as much as men, have contributed to the sales of "hard-boiled" fiction in our time. Judging from the reaction of service men to such a book as Norman Mailer's *The Naked and the Dead*, elsewhere noted in these pages, I venture the guess that women readers helped substantially to place it on the best-seller lists. I have no doubt there are still editors who share the illusion of the writer I have quoted; but I think they might be surprised at the response if they were to conceive of their feminine audience as human beings whose horizons, as well as their faces, have been lifted, rather than as members merely of one of the two well-established sexes.

No statistics, so far as I am aware, are available, but it would be interesting to know just how large a proportion of the novelists writing in the United States today are women. Certainly half; perhaps more. If you glance at the best-seller lists for any month, you are reasonably sure to find as many women as men listed under the fiction heading. The bulk of non-fiction, whether on the best-seller lists or off, is still written by men, but the feminine invasion in the fields of biography, history, world affairs, science, and so on, steadily grows in strength. Probably the best-known contemporary writer in the field of anthropology today is a woman, Margaret Mead; one of the best-known popularizers of modern psychology is Dr. Karen Horney. Two of the keenest minds and most expressive pens in the field of literary criticism belong to Rebecca West and Mary Colum. High on the list of economists who can use words as well as graphs is the name of Barbara Ward, one of the editors of the world's foremost periodical in its field, the *Economist* of London. The Pulitzer prizes for biography went in two recent successive years to women.

But it is in fiction that the women have made themselves chiefly felt. They have, of course, long outnumbered men as readers of novels; and now, by all the signs and portents, they are well on the way to becoming the novel's chief producers. Even in those departments of fiction where one might reasonably expect men to predominate—in the mystery and the Western story, for example—women have been coming increasingly to the fore. The names of Agatha Christie and Dorothy Sayers, to mention only two outstanding concocters of the whodunit, are on a par with those of any male contemporary; even the horror story has its feminine practitioners. Yet perhaps these facts are not so strange, considering that there have been almost as many famous and devilishly efficient female murderers as men.

For a long time now, women have disported themselves in the field of the historical novel, and they have themselves contributed not a few of those high-bosomed hussies who have recently been taking the center of the stage in our historical fiction. Was it not, indeed, a young woman named Kathleen Winsor who gave the hard-dying wave a new impetus with her *Forever Amber*, as it was a far more literate and historically minded member of her sex, Margaret Mitchell, who wrote the most readable of all Civil War romances? And still another, Esther Forbes, who has been acclaimed as one of those writers who are lifting the historical novel back to its rightful place as a commendable form of fiction?

Now there is nothing new, certainly, about the ability of women to write fiction. Among all the arts, the one in which they have long achieved the greatest distinction is the art of the novel. There have been good, and even great women poets, from Sappho down to Edith Sitwell, but there is little doubt, I think, that an even more imposing roster can be drawn from the novelists. Women's record is more impressive by far in the literary arts than in other creative fields. It would be a simple matter, for example, to list many good painters and sculptors among women, but impossible to name one of unquestionably first rank. And there has never been a great woman composer, a great woman architect.

Women's eminence in fiction goes back a long time. They were among the first writers of one of the earliest forms of fiction—that same field in which their recent exploits have just been noted—the historical romance. A Frenchwoman, Madeleine de Scudéry, living in the seventeenth century, wrote the best-known tale of this kind in her time. What literary historians like to describe as the first psychological novel was Madame de la Fayette's *La Princesse de Clèves,* published in 1678. This is the book to which Somerset Maugham recently referred as one which any Frenchman, drawing up a list of the world's best novels, would unhesitatingly include. It is a curious fact, incidentally, that in spite of this pioneering of theirs in fiction, the number of Frenchwomen who have since distinguished themselves in the novel is far fewer than the English and ourselves can show—and I am not forgetting either George Sand in the past or Colette in the present. Finally, it was a woman, Aphra Behn, who in the seventeenth century wrote what has been called the first humanitarian novel in English.

My mention of these facts is merely to remind you

that women, although in fewer numbers than now, have always played an important part in the writing of fiction. And, after all, why not? Fiction's chief concern, apart from its primary function of telling a story, is with the relations of human beings to one another—and have not these relations always been a prime interest of women, whatever their degree of culture or their place in the social scale? Might not one even make out a good case for the proposition that more women than men (excluding, of course, the natural politicians) are interested in people as people? And isn't the capacity for sympathetic understanding generally conceived of as being stronger in the average woman than in the average male, and isn't that capacity a very important factor in the writing of psychologically sound fiction?

It is true, perhaps, that this capacity for sympathy (not always, one must admit, generously extended toward members of her own sex) is an asset to the woman novelist only up to a certain point, beyond which it becomes a handicap. For it may be argued with more than a little cogency that the majority of women are unable to see men objectively, particularly when their emotions are involved. And since so much of fiction that deals with the relations between men and women has a strong autobiographical base, the emotional factor often plays too great a part in the woman novelist's handling of her male characters. Men writers are betrayed in this fashion also—a fact to which I shall return—but not, I think, in the same degree. I once heard a successful woman novelist argue that men, speaking generally, were able to pass through their relationships with women relatively unscathed, because so much of their inner lives, their compulsions and drives, remains independent of the sexual relationship. Consequently, in their fiction, they are better able to portray the opposite sex as it actually is. Women, on the other hand, whose identification with the object of their love is a so much deeper, life-embracing experience, are more likely to reveal in their fiction their fuller emotional involvement.

As I have already remarked, no generalizations are more to be mistrusted than those made about the nature of men versus the nature of women. Certainly one could compile a formidable list of male novelists, beginning with Scott and coming down to Sinclair Lewis and Ernest Hemingway, who have been prevailingly inept in their female characterizations, offering us creatures of fantasy molded not from the stuff of actuality, but out of their hearts' desire.

Indeed, I think there has been a growing tendency, in American fiction by male novelists particularly, for heroines to assume one of two predominant forms: either that of the docile but passionate dream-girl who lives to do her lord and master's bidding, and whom we might describe as the nice but negative type; or her more positively motivated sister—the one with the Toni—who shares with dogs of the female gender a short and somewhat unpleasant-sounding name. The dream-girl and the bitch have, of course, been familiar types ever since men began to seek compensation for their frustrations through the medium of fiction writing, but formerly the variations from type were more numerous, and certainly the characters of the second category were once more engaging creatures than their excessively hard-boiled descendants of the present day. Defoe's Roxana or Moll Flanders, for example, would unquestionably have been pleasanter company than that thoroughly obnoxious female whose reactions to life were clinically observed by Mr. John O'Hara in *A Rage to Live*.

Hemingway's most credible women characters have been Lady Brett Ashley of *The Sun Also Rises*, perhaps the most sharply defined portrait of the bitch-type drawn by an American male novelist, and Pilár of *For Whom the Bell Tolls*, an earthy woman with a man's strength, who yet thought of herself as a woman made for men; at the opposite pole, he has brought the dream-girl, beginning with Catherine Barkley of *A Farewell to Arms*, on through the little cropped-head of *For Whom the Bell Tolls*, to a conclusion so extreme, in the person of the young Contessa of *Across the River and Into the Trees*, that it is impossible to imagine a more docile, yet passionate creature. She has become merely a handsome receptacle for the male's yearnings and the mirror for his narcissism.

When I set forth these views in a column in the *Times*,

one of my correspondents, a woman, suggested that in the type of the second category—the one favored by Mr. O'Hara and other so-called realists, as well as by all historical novelists of the Thoracic School—there may be seen emerging a variation from type, still somewhat amorphous, but destined to develop into a full-blown projection of the "new woman." Even in her cruder manifestations, even when she is luridly amoral, thought my correspondent, she symbolizes independence and a woman's ability to think and decide for herself. "She may be crude, violent, flashy, venomous," wrote Mrs. Brown, "but she is not docile." My correspondent went on to remark that this new figure is still something of a stranger to the author as well as to the world. She is likely to be a career girl, attempting to adjust her ambitions to her natural impulses and desires. "Her position in society," she wrote, is paradoxical. Wanting marriage and children, she does not want the deadly monotony of housekeeping. She does not want to obliterate her ego in repetitious slavery. Education has shown her the way toward self-realization, but not the vehicle for traveling this harsh and challenging road. So this heroine may be cynical, disillusioned, shocking to her bewildered male who, in his heart, still searches for the Catherines. Countless young authors have tried to present her, but rarely has she been properly interpreted."

Watching her emerge in the first novels of this post-war generation, my correspondent observed that she is usually too emphatic about her independence, and sometimes downright masculine in the conduct of her personal life. "Yet she is capable of moral concepts, and frequently has a rigid sense of honor. Her feminine qualities have suffered, in her long struggle for adjustment. But she is searching still for a full and happy realization of her essential womanly self." Mrs. Brown thought that in time she will replace the Catherines as the ideal heroine, because, for better or worse, the Catherines grow steadily fewer; that as her adjustment is completed, this girl of the new age will grow in charm and will lose her cynicism; that men will come to love her for herself, and not for her reflection of themselves. Certainly I hope so, but she has still a long, hard road ahead; and even though the Catherines and the Contessas may join the dodo in extinction, we may count, I am convinced, on their continuance in fiction, if not in life.

The fact is that for satirical or dispassionately realistic portraits of women—the kind of portrait achieved by Balzac, for example, in *Cousine Bette*—you must, in the American novel, turn to the work of the women themselves: to such writers as Willa Cather and Ellen Glasgow. None of our male novelists has been able to create the counterpart in this respect, of Miss Cather's Mrs. Forrester in *A Lost Lady*, or Miss Glasgow's Eva Birdsong in *The Sheltered Life*. Henry James was, it is true, in a bloodless fashion at home in the intricacies of feminine behavior, and Howells, within the bounds of his imposed taboos and his natural reticence, maintained his balance. David Graham Phillips, a novelist who might have gone much farther had he lived longer, gave token of his capacity in *Susan Lennox: Her Fall and Rise*. Nor are there any memorable women in our earlier fiction. *The Scarlet Letter* is a great book, but Hawthorne's Hester Prynne was a wraith. Melville did not write of women, and they played but little part in the fictional world of Mark Twain. For Dreiser women were little more than objects of male desire, as they are for Hemingway. Whatever the value of his fiction as social criticism, the characters of John Dos Passos, whether women or men, have always been merely two-dimensional. The women of Sinclair Lewis, with the exception of Fran Dodsworth, who has always seemed to me his most fully realized woman character, rather than the more generally favored Leora Arrowsmith, have been simply projections of the male yearnings for a creature who would combine in the one person the roles of mistress, wife, and friend. Steinbeck's one memorable woman character is Ma Joad, and she, more than anything else, was a personification of the maternal principle, of woman's role as the binding force and preserver of family unity. Scott Fitzgerald's girls were no more than pretty iridescent bubbles blown into the air of the mad Twenties.

Sometimes these dream-girls who throng the pages of American men novelists achieve a kind of spurious reality from the backgrounds against which they appear. Suppose we return for a moment to Hemingway's women, since it is he who has, as I have already remarked, carried that sort of projection to its ultimate conclusion. Consider the "little rabbit" of *For Whom the Bell Tolls*; if it weren't for that cropped head of hers I should have great difficulty in visualizing her at all, nor can I imagine how she might conduct herself in any situation more complex than that offered by crawling into a sleeping bag. We don't know her, although we do remember her —but not for the same reasons that we remember Becky Sharp or Anna Karenina or Cousine Bette or Scarlett O'Hara, who, I believe, is one of the most completely created women in modern fiction. We remember Maria or Catherine Barkley because the situations in which they were placed were made extraordinarily vivid for us by a very skilled writer. Hemingway is a master of mood (which is why he is a better short-story writer than he is a novelist), and we remember Maria and Catherine because we cannot disassociate them from the blowing of the bridge or from the walk home in the rain.

Even in the case of so great a novel as *The Scarlet Letter*, the same point may be made, if not as fully, because Arthur Dimmesdale and Hester Prynne are more deeply realized as individuals (even though I have called Hester a wraith) than are the Hemingway characters. Nevertheless, they are to a greater degree than most of the memorable characters in fiction, merely symbolic figures who take on great dimensions simply because of the intense strength of the scenes in which they are depicted and the powerful moral overtones of the theme in which they are used. They are not, that is to say, realistically projected characters in anything like the degree to which, for example, Anna and Levin are in *Anna Karenina*. Though their reactions to the circumstances in which they find themselves are more deeply explored than those of the lovers in *A Farewell to Arms,* we do not know the separate elements of their characters and temperaments as we know those of many lesser figures in fiction.

The projection of the dream-girl by men novelists seems always more marked among those writers whose quality we regard as outstandingly masculine, the writers whose appeal is regarded as primarily to men—the Fieldings, the Scotts, the Kiplings, the Lewises, and the Hemingways. Their women characters are not seen from the inside, but from the plane of very sufficient maleness. A good case could be made for the contention that, with some exceptions, women novelists have been more perceptive in their handling of male characters than have men in their portraits of women. But is it strange that this should be so? Women, from the time of the cave dwellers, have made the study of the opposite sex their chief occupation; they had to, in self-defense, if for no other reason. Men, on the other hand, unless possessed of natural understanding, like Tolstoy, have been content to look down from their assured positions of male superiority and to shake their heads over the incomprehensible behavior of the other sex.

Readers of Jane Austen always wonder how Jane, a spinster living a sheltered life in provincial England, and in a time when spinsterhood was a much more confined condition than it is today, came to know so much about the male. It was G. K. Chesterton who pointed out that when, in *Pride and Prejudice*, Jane Austen has Darcy confessing his faults, and makes him say, "I have been a selfish being all my life, in practice *though not in theory*," she comes pretty close to setting down a complete confession of the average intelligent male. Yet it is possible, granted the knowledge and skill with which Jane Austen wrote about men (she could not, of course, in her time, have told all the truth, even if she knew it), to mention other accomplished women novelists whose touch was much less sure.

Suppose we take, for example, the case of Willa Cather, whose portraits of members of her own sex are so memorable. One has the feeling, in reading her, that she is handling men from a safe distance; she seldom gets deep under the skin, and is at her best, when portraying the male, if her subject is seen from far off, like her Archbishop in the old Southwest. Ellen Glasgow, on the other hand, knew as much, and, in some respects, I think, a little more than Jane. She was especially adept in her drawing of aging men, and in all the work of her mature years, she wrote of the male sex completely without illusion. So, too, at times, did Edith Wharton, and Elizabeth Madox Roberts, whose best work should be much better known that it is, had her moments of acute penetration. Three scenes of hers—one in *The Time of Man,* another in *The Great Meadow,* and a third in *My Heart and My Flesh*—in their deep understanding of male-female relationships, stand with the best that American or any other fiction can show. Jonas confessing his infidelity to Ellen in *The Time of Man,* Diony choosing between her new husband and the one given up for dead, in *The Great Meadow,* and Theodosia saying goodbye to Albert in *My Heart and My Flesh,* are masterly in their grasp of both masculine and feminine psychology.

And certainly the contribution of women to fiction has not been merely in the direction of introducing a woman's point of view—or what is generally conceived of as a woman's point of view. Thus, was it not Jane Austen who, more than any other single writer, rescued the English novel from the maudlin romanticism into which it had fallen during the closing years of the eighteenth century? And was it not another woman, Ellen Glasgow, who in our own time, made the first move to rescue the fiction of the South from its immersion in rose water? Also, is it not yielding to a treacherous generalization when we say of some novelist that she "writes like a woman?" I believe it to be as insubstantial a characterization as to say of some one that he or she drives like a woman. Who has not seen an exasperated wife snatch a hammer from the fumbling hands of her spouse, and how often the business sagacity in a marriage falls on the distaff side!

Do not women more often appear to write "like women" because of their subject matter than because of a "feminine quality" in their style? The world of which Jane Austen wrote is undeniably a woman's world; it is compounded of those small, sharply restricted interests which made up the sum of living for those women of her period and place who seldom had the opportunity of looking over the walls of a rigid provincial society. Suppose Jane had been born in 1900, and had shared the freedom of movement and experience common to her generation; would she have written quite as she did, and would her novels have been as obviously feminine? Jane had the outward-looking eye, and no novelist, whether man or woman, concealed the subjective content present in all fiction better than she. To choose a more recent example, yet one not greatly affected by the altered relationships of men and women or the widened horizons of her own sex—think for a moment of George Eliot. She is less read today than Jane, probably because she lacked Jane's wit and also because of her insistent moralizing. But her penetration of both men's and women's behavior was acute, and if we did not know her sex we could not definitely distinguish *Middlemarch,* her best and most ambitious work, from that of her male contemporaries. And on the reverse side of the coin, think for a moment of a writer so predominantly masculine as Kipling; if a woman would not have written *Plain Tales from the Hills*, surely *The Brushwood Boy* might have come from a feminine pen. Nor am I at all sure that a woman could not have written Hemingway's best short story, *The Snows of Kilimanjaro*.

When one enters the field of poetry, the dividing lines become even more shadowy. When Anne Bradstreet, one of the earliest of American writers, delivers herself of a reflective poem like "Contemplations," she is indistinguishable from the male poets of her period who wrote in similar vein. When Edna St. Vincent Millay wrote her lyrics of forgotten loves, she was unmistakably a woman writing, but was her sex so readily identifiable when she wrote her philosophical sonnets?

All I am suggesting is that wherever writing is not so patently subjective as to reveal the writer's personal link to his or her material, wherever the choice of subject matter does not set up a plain marker, it becomes increasingly difficult, as wider areas of life are shared between men and women, to distinguish the work of one from the other.

It is incontrovertibly true that, so far, the greatest novelists have been men. But whenever you have man of supreme ability in the novel—a Stendhal, a Balzac, a Dickens, a Dostoevsky, a Tolstoy—you have a man whose mentality and temperament contain certain so-called feminine traits, especially the qualities of intuition and sympathy that we ordinarily associate with the more realistic sex (for men contribute by far the larger number of the world's dreamers and most flagrantly impractical idealists). It is the possession of these qualities of intuition and sympathy, combined with those in which men are commonly considered as stronger—logic, constructive power, imaginative grasp, emotional detachment—that has made it possible for men to occupy the first rank.

A novelist like Tolstoy was able, like Shakespeare, to write about women with as much understanding as he did about men because, although he was certainly no member of an indeterminate sex, but on the contrary, a lusty lover of women, there were these feminine components in his mentality and nature. I think, as a matter of fact, that you will find this tincture of the feminine in almost every supreme artist in whatever field, though it is doubtful if it applies in comparable degree to the great composers or architects, even to the great sculptors and painters, because in these arts so much rests upon the capacity for abstract thought and that constructive grasp which seems absent from the predominantly feminine mind. It is significant, surely, that no woman has ever created a philosophical system, a task for which these capacities are indispensable.

Virginia Woolf had a theory, which she set forth in *A Room of Her Own,* that too many men novelists in our time are writing with only one side of their brains—the masculine side. (It is true, of course, that some have little or none of the other.) It was this fusion of male and female characteristics, she thought, of which Coleridge was thinking when he said that a great mind is androgynous. He certainly did not mean, she reflected, "that it is a mind which has any special sympathy with women; a mind that takes up their cause or devotes itself to their interpretation. Perhaps the androgynous mind is less likely to make these distinctions than the single-sexed mind. He meant, perhaps, that the androgynous mind is resonant and porous; that it transmits emotion without impediment; that it is naturally creative, incandescent and undivided. In fact, one goes back to Shakespeare's mind as the type of the androgynous, of the man-womanly mind, though it would be impossible to say what Shakespeare thought of women."

This capacity which Shakespeare had was contrasted by Coleridge with Fielding's lack of it when he compared their handling of character. He found that Fielding, for whom he had great admiration as a writer, praising highly the truth and humor he arrived at by observation, was wholly dependent upon what he had actually observed. He pointed out that where Fielding could not help himself by copying what he had seen, where it was necessary that "something should take place, some words be spoken, or some object described which he could not have witnessed his soliloquies, for example, or the interview between the hero Tom Jones and Sophia Western before the reconciliation," he becomes unnatural and forced and lacking in psychological truth. It was, on the other hand, the measure of Shakespeare's completeness that no situation seemed alien to him, no character closed to him, whether of man or of woman.

Mrs. Woolf surmised that today men are writing more and more frequently with only the male part of their brains because we are living in an extraordinarily sex-conscious period, and that, for this reason, virility has become very self-conscious. It seems to me a reasonable supposition. That self-consciousness is fed from so many and such omnipresent sources: in our advertising, in the verbal and pictorial content of our newspapers and magazines, and in the movies. The constant and exaggerated stimulation of sex-consciousness is inescapable. And certainly no period has been so self-consciously insistent that certain books and certain writers are definitely masculine or feminine in their appeal. I cannot imagine that the Thurber cartoons, or the Thurber thesis of the war between the sexes, could at any previous time have had the edge and point that they hold for us today.

It seems to me that, in the present state of flux in which the relation between the sexes is, the character of fiction in the immediate and more distant future must inevitably reflect more fully than it has the altered condition of women, their attitude toward men, and that of men toward them. Certainly it it reasonable to expect that with the growth of woman's first-hand knowledge of activities from which she had formerly been excluded, as her participation in them continues to grow, as she comes more completely to understand the motives that prompt men in their relations between themselves her scope and insight as a novelist will be still further widened and deepened. And is it too much to hope that as men come more fully and in larger numbers to appreciate the difficult position in which women today find themselves, torn as they are between their instinctual drives to fulfill themselves as females and their compulsion to realize themselves more fully as human beings without regard to sex, men will broaden and deepen their own insights in the fiction which they write?

The reconciliation of masculine and feminine qualities that has been made so difficult by the economic and social pressures under which we live must, it seems to me, inject itself more and more into all creative writing that undertakes adequately to reflect our time. Men and women today stand at a kind of crossroads in their relationship. Women won't and probably can't go back to the safe but irksome Victorian enclosure; they are faced with finding the middle path, if any. All that inner turmoil, from which no thinking woman in our time is free, will necessarily be reflected more and more in the books she writes, particularly the novels.

Precisely two hundred years ago, Samuel Richardson, who knew his way about in the mazes of feminine psychology as few writers before or after him, had this to say in a letter to Lady Bradshaigh: "Such is the nature of woman, if she be not a vixen indeed, that if the men sets out right with her; if he lets her early know that he is her lord, and that she is but his vassal; that that he has a stronger sense of his prerogative than of her merit and beauty; she will succumb: and after a few struggles, a few tears, will make him a more humble, a more passive wife, for his insolent bravery, and high opinion of himself." By and large, that was true when Richardson wrote it, and it is true of many women today; but their number grows fewer. The changes have been wide and deep.

But there is as yet little general comprehension among our writers of the fact that women, in their struggle toward readjustment—a struggle which men forced upon them when they brought the industrial age into being—have now arrived at a crucial point, beyond which they cannot go without men's understanding and help. Their situation has been penetratingly described by Haniel Long. I quote from *A Letter to St. Augustine:* "The unavailingness of the masculine mind operating without the feminine is written large in the condition of today. Woman's reverence for life and her powers of nourishing do not balance man's instinct for power. They are not allowed to. The way has not been prepared for them to do so. Even in the hearts of some women the clearing of the way has only just begun. Men who find their maleness bankrupt as a spiritual force, long for the assistance of women to whom peace means, as Elin Wagner said, not only 'peace on earth, but peace with the earth.'

". . . To help each other the sexes must know each other. Patriarchy is done for and no good. It is true that we may yet see woman in her negative as well as positive aspects as we have never dreamt we should see her. She is being born again, is delivering herself of herself.

"We think of God as male instead of female because during the patriarchal age we could not imagine God not being a man. But now that patriarchy has outlived its practicability and is following matriarchy into oblivion, and a new age, which might be called filiarchy, the age of the child, begins, we feel that the Divine Spirit is more and more animated by the maternal."

Through many centuries it has been difficult for men to see women other than as creatures existing on earth for their comfort, pleasure, and convenience. They have not been seen adequately as individual human personalities. One indication of this was remarked by Edith Hamilton in her *Spokesmen of God*, when she observed that "the Bible is the only literature in the world up to our own century which looks at women as human beings, no better and no worse than men. The Old Testament writers considered them just as impartially as they did men, free from prejudice and even from condescension."

The theme of reconciliation between men and women must, it seems to me, be one of the great themes which writers will approach during the remainder of this century. Like the question of the survival of individual freedom in modern society, or the quest for the recovery of faith, it is one of the basic problems of twentieth-century man—one of the three the solution of which is essential to the continuance of both his material and spiritual development. A great deal has been written on the fringes of this question, on the obvious results to date of what we refer to as women's emancipation. But there has been little writing of a creative kind which has really come to grips with the matter of how important the changing relationship between men and women is; little which can be described as constructive.

The seeds for such writing were sown nearly half a century ago by Rainer Maria Rilke, in the series of letters to a young friend subsequently published as *Letters to a Young Poet*. In one of them he remarked that we were only just beginning to look upon the relation of one individual to a second without prejudice and realistically, and then went on to say:

"Girls and women in their new, their own unfolding will but in passing be imitators of masculine vices and virtues and repeaters of masculine professions. After the uncertainty of such transitions it will become apparent that women only went through the whole range and variety of these (often ridiculous) disguises in order to clean their own most characteristic nature of the distorting influence of the other sex. Women, in whom life lingers and dwells more immediately, more fruitfully and more confidently, must naturally have become fundamentally riper people, more human people, than man who is easy-going, by the weight of no fruit of his body pulled down below the surface of life, and who, presumptuous and hasty, undervalues what he thinks he loves.

"This humanity of women, carried out in suffering and humiliation, will then, when in the commutations of her external situation she will have stripped off the conventions of being only feminine, come to light, and those men, who do not yet feel it approaching today will be astonished and stunned by it. Some day (and of this, particularly in the Northern countries, reliable signs already speak), some day there will be girls and women whose name will no longer signify merely an opposite of the masculine, but something in itself, something that makes one think, not of any complement and limit, but of life and existence: the female human being.

"This advance will (at first much against the will of the men who have been outstripped) change the experiencing of love, which is now full of error, will alter it from the ground up, reshape it into a relation that is meant to be one human being to another, no longer of man to woman. And this more human love (that will fulfill itself, infinitely considerate and gentle, and good and clear in binding and releasing) will resemble that which we are with struggle and endeavor preparing, the love that consists in this, that two solitudes protect and touch and greet each other."

Perhaps, who knows, we shall come round in the end to the concept ascribed to Aristophanes in the *Sympo-*

68

sium of Plato, that "human nature was originally one and we were a whole, and the desire and pursuit of the whole is called love." Or, in mythological terms, that the gods separated man from women, and that they have been trying, ever since, to effect their reunion.

"The wise man," remarks André Gide in that book of delicate and sometimes deep perceptions, *The Fruits of the Earth*, "is he who constantly wonders afresh." He might better, perhaps, have written "fortunate" for "wise," for the wisdom, it seems to me, should be assigned rather to result than cause. They are the lucky ones in whom the sense of wonder and delight are kept forever fresh; it is they who are the true darlings of the gods. For theirs is only rarely an acquired capacity, summoned by reason and maintained by practice; it is a gift far more to be treasured than the proverbial silver spoon. Its possession carries with it one of the few guarantees, aside from those ancient familiars, death and taxes, which human life affords. For its possessor can never be poor in the things that matter most; for him the world is always being born again.

Two kinds of people have it most: those with simple, unquestioning natures, in whom life runs a natural and uncomplicated course, as in the animals who have stayed within the frame of nature as we ourselves have not; and, somewhat paradoxically, those at the other end of the human scale, those most highly organized individuals among whom are found the supreme artists of the race. It is the possession of the Shakespeares, the Leonardos, the Balzacs, the Goethes, the Tolstoys.

It was Kenneth Grahame, who will live forever blessed as the author of *The Wind in the Willows*, who once spoke a few words that might well be framed above every writer's desk: "The most priceless possession of the human race is the wonder of the world." The remark was made in conversation with Clayton Hamilton, who had asked Grahame why he had written almost entirely about children and animals. It is not often that we have from a great writer (and within the limits he set for himself I think the adjective may be applied to Grahame with assurance) a satisfying explanation of why he wrote as he did. There is no reason, of course, why a creative artist should feel any need to supplement the testimony his work itself provides. As often as not, if what he wrote had its roots in an urgent inner compulsion, as most books worth reading have, the perceptive reader can readily and justly supply the answer himself.

But to be fully understood in its relation to his work and in its application to my theme, Grahame's words need to be supplemented by those which followed them: "Latterly," he explained, "the utmost endeavors of mankind have been directed toward the dissipation of that wonder. . . . Science analyzes everything to its component parts and neglects to put them together again. . . .

"Granted that the average man may live for seventy years, it is a fallacy to assume that his life from sixty to seventy is more important than his life from five to fifteen. Children are not merely people; they are the only really living people that have been left to us in an over-weary world. Any normal child will instinctively agree with your own American poet, Walt Whitman, when he said: 'To me, every hour of the day and night is an unspeakably perfect miracle.'

"In my tales about children, I have tried to show that their simple acceptance of the mood of wonderment, their readiness to welcome a perfect miracle at any hour of the day or night, is a thing more precious than any of the labored acquisitions of adult mankind."

And as for the animals, Grahame said he wrote about them in *The Wind in the Willows*—that book so full of wisdom applicable to mankind—because "Every animal by instinct lives according to its nature. Thereby he lives wisely, and betters the tradition of mankind. No animal is ever tempted to belie his nature. No animal, in other words, knows how to tell a lie. Every animal is honest. Every animal is straightforward. Every animal is true —and is, therefore, according to his nature, both beautiful and good."

But the essence of Grahame's approach to his work

is contained in that first remark—"The most priceless possession of the human race is the wonder of the world." It is the first possession that all of us have—as everyone knows who has watched a baby discovering his world— and the first of importance that most of us lose. And how rare, and how prized, are those few writers who, because their perception of the wonder of the world is genuine and constantly renewed, are of help to us in retaining and renewing our own! They are not only the writers of the immortal stories of childhood; they are the truly great poets; they are the novelists from whom we derive a fuller sense of the meaning of human experience.

"The wonder of the world"—it lies at the heart of all great literature, from Homer down. When we find it in a book, as when we encounter it in life, we are released, for the time being, from the choking grip of sophistication and the dead hand of cynicism. But though there are those who keep the sense of wonder and are able to convey it to us, yet even for them it is a fitful, intermittent light—this light that illuminates what H. M. Tomlinson called "the magic moment." There is a passage in *The Sea and the Jungle*, one of the most magical of travel books, in which Tomlinson transfixes its quality. He speaks of the magic moment in relation to travel, but the application of his words is to all moments in which the sense of wonder is stirred and held:

"I myself," he writes, "learned that the treasures found

74

in travel, the chance rewards of travel which make it worth while, cannot be accounted for beforehand and seldom are matters a listener would care to hear about afterward; for they have no substance. They are no matter. They are untranslatable from their time and place; and like the man who unwittingly lies down to sleep in the tumulus where the little people dance on midsummer night and dreams that in the place where man has never been his pockets were filled with fairy gold, waking to find pebbles there instead, so the traveler cannot prove the dreams he had, showing us only pebbles when he tries. Such fair things cannot be taken from the magic moment. They are but filmy, high in the ceiling of your thoughts for so brief a while, rosy and sunlit by the chance of the light, transitory, melting as you watch."

Now Tomlinson was naturally thinking of what he had seen and felt on his journey up the Amazon, but what he says about the treasures found in travel holds true, in varying measure, for all our moments of heightened experience. And too often, when we try to communicate what the moment meant to us, we realize we are offering pebbles in place of the fairy gold we found.

That is the eternal problem of every writer, even of the most gifted, unless he works on a purely factual level. It is, indeed, the ever-present problem of every artist. Always there is something he has felt intensely, so much so that he must find expression for what has moved him. And, almost always, it is a form of beauty. That is a word which, unfortunately, has become suspect in our day, but those who shy away from it have usually not stopped to think how wide a word it is.

For all of us are dependent on beauty, in one form or another, for our deepest satisfactions to a greater degree than most of us are aware. Sometimes we call it by another name; we speak of precision, or justice, or logic, but they are all diverse aspects of the same face for which we are always looking. Beauty in one form or another appeals to the most matter-of-fact of human beings, even those so unimaginative as not to be conscious of what it is that stirs them. There is beauty in the strategy of war, though its product is antithesis. There can be beauty in a lawyer's brief, in the technique of a surgical operation, in the blueprint of an engineer.

That was a profoundly true, even if unprovable, observation of Walter Bagehot: "There is hardly a human life which would not have been different if the idea of beauty in the mind of the man who had lived it had been different." That sentence, I think, provides as good a cue as any to the importance of beauty as a factor in our lives. Might not one even say that the fearfully distorted vision which erected itself in the disordered mind of Hitler was brought into being in obedience to this universal human need, this craving which can assert itself in strange and terrible forms? May not one, in cool dispassion, think of Hitler not merely as the thwarted artist of his youth, but also as the grown man who, in the New Order of his dream (nightmare, if you prefer), found the promise of fulfilment in the quest for beauty which had eluded him in his futile dabblings as a painter?

John Galsworthy, who, though he missed the final heights of artistic expression, was one of the most sensitively endowed writers of our time, somewhere spoke of the moments of beauty we perceive and feel, as "the drops of rain that keep the human spirit from death by drought." With that remark I am brought back to Tomlinson's feeling about the unrecoverability of the magic moments of travel. It is the function of poetry, more than any other art, perhaps, to capture and preserve such moments, whether they are experienced in travel or at home. Poetry, at its best, succeeds in keeping the fairy gold untransmuted into baser form. That which is "but filmy, high in the ceiling of your thoughts for so brief a while, rosy and sunlit by the chance of the light, transitory, melting as you watch," is precisely what poetry is sometimes able to catch and hold.

In a lecture delivered at Oxford some years ago, Benedetto Croce said: "If, then, poetry is intuition and expression, the fusion of sound and imagery, what is the material which takes on the form of sound and imagery? It is the whole man: the man who thinks and wills, and loves, and hates; who is strong and weak, sublime and pathetic, good and wicked; man in the exultation and agony of living; and together with the man, integral with him, is all nature in its perpetual labor of evolution. But

77

the thoughts and actions and emotions of life, when sub-limated to the subject-matter of poetry, are no longer the thought that judges, the action eventually carried out, the good and evil, or the joy and pain actually done or suffered. They are all now simply passions and feelings immediately assuaged and calmed, and transfigured in imagery.

"That is the magic of poetry, the union of calm and tumult, of passionate impulse with the controlling mind which controls by contemplating. It is the triumph of contemplation, but a triumph still shaken by past battle, with its foot upon a living though vanquished foe. Poetic genius chooses a strait path in which passion is calmed and calm is passionate; a path that has on one side merely natural feeling, and on the other the reflection and criticism which is twice removed from nature; a path from which minor talents find it but too easy to slip into an art either convulsed and distorted by passion, or void of passion and guided by principles of the understanding."

Is it not this union of calm and tumult of which Croce spoke that poetry in our time has so largely lost and has thus surrendered the best that poetry is capable of giving—that "momentary stay against confusion" of which Robert Frost has spoken when he said that a poem begins in delight and ends in wisdom—at least a minor clarification of life? That clarification can be reached only out of the union of tumult and calm. But when poetry is guided only by principles of the understanding, as so much poetry has been during the past quarter century the magic is too often absent, and we have only what, nine times out of ten, could have been better said in prose. Too much modern poetry has failed to start with Tomlinson's "magic moment" or Frost's "delight." It has tried to do by purely rational means what must be done by thought and emotion together.

Those moments which Tomlinson called "magic" are described by his contemporary, C. E. Montague, as "unaccountable." The phrase is used in *Disenchantment*, the book in which Montague, one of the most felicitous of latter-day English essayists, gave reflective expression to the disillusionment that that came with World War I. It is a book that makes suggestive reading today, not only for the likenesses of mood which it depicts, but for the differences as well. They can be felt fully, perhaps, only by those who have lived through the impact of both conflicts. This was made especially clear to me recently when reading the reviews of a new biography of Rupert Brooke. Those critics whose knowledge of the world in which Brooke grew up is at second-hand have, unless they possess unusually sensitive antennae, little conception of how closely the emotions to which Brooke gave expression in his war poetry were duplicated among his less articulate contemporaries. His poetry has lost its savor for the generation which fought World War II, but its feeling was, in its own time, genuine. The emotions out of which that poetry was written are all but incomprehensible to the inheritors of the disillusion that came with World War I.

But I have strayed from Montague's "unaccountable moments." In writing of them he had, in high degree you will observe, certain qualities that are almost always present in masters of the art of informal discourse. He had a strong sense of and respect for the incommunicable, and he knew there are matters that can be conveyed, if at all, only by indirection. But what is most important, he was vibrantly aware of the significance that seemingly little things can assume. (Wasn't there a collection of essays by Chesterton called *Tremendous Trifles?*)

And so he wrote: "When you think of the youth that you have lost, the times when it seems to you now that life was most poignantly good may not be the ones when everything seemed at the time to go well with your plans, and the world, as they say, to be at your feet; rather some few unaccountable moments when nothing took place that was out of the way and yet some word of a friend's, or a look on the face of the sky, the taste of a glass of spring water, the plash of laughter and oars heard across midsummer meadows at night raised the soul of enjoyment within you to strangely higher powers of itself. That spirit bloweth and is still; it will not rise for all our whistling or keep a time-table; no wine that we know can give us anything more than a fugitive caricature of its ecstasies. When it has blown free we remember it always, and know, without proof, that while the rapture was there we were not drunk, but wise; that for a moment some intervening darkness had thinned and we were seeing further than we can now see into the heart of life."

No writer is worth his salt who does not keep fresh in his mind the knowledge that the revealing incident, the illuminating flash, is, as often as not, unattended by portents or the roll of drums. Its coming is unheralded, and its passage as swift as that of the Perseids that have this week been slashing across the night sky. And it is one of the smaller ironies of life that "the times when it seems to you now that life was most poignantly good may not be the ones when everything seemed at the time to go well with your plans."

The Declaration of Independence is, by and large, a noble document, but that betraying phrase, "the pursuit of happiness," leaves no room for doubt that there were lacks even in the remarkable versatility of Thomas Jefferson. No true-blown essayist could have written it, for he knows, if he knows nothing else, that what Montague refers to as "the soul of enjoyment within you" is something that "bloweth and is still." Of one thing we can be certain: that it will not "rise for our whistling." I can conceive of no more improbable case-history than that of a man or woman who pursued happiness and found it. Happiness and calamity are twins in unexpectedness.

Closely akin to those "unaccountable moments" is the capacity for enjoyment of little things, of which Montague has written more perceptively than almost any writer

I know. That capacity, which everyone has in childhood, and which is being lost at an accelerating rate in the world of today, is perhaps the surest guarantor of the "unaccountable moments." It is a capacity, as Montague points out, which in turn rests upon our ability to take delight in a thing for its own sake, and not as a means to some other end, as "a child in the full health of his mind will put his hand flat on the summer turf, feel it, and give a little shiver of private glee at the elastic firmness of the globe. He is not thinking of how well it will do for some game or to feed sheep upon." And I share Montague's belief that "The right education, if we could find it, would work up this creative faculty of delight into all its branching possibilities of knowledge, wisdom and nobility. Of all three it is the beginning, condition, or raw material."

At this point I fancy I can hear distinct mutterings, with definite overtones of imprecation, directed at me by those readers who may feel that I have been indulging in what might be described as cloud-treading. Indeed, my innocent observations concerning what seems to me the fallacious nature of Jefferson's apparent belief in the snareability of happiness, called forth, on their initial appearance in the *Times*, a hotly indignant letter from one correspondent, who took me to task for overlooking the fact that whether or not Jefferson was aware of the unbiddable aspect of happiness, he did hold at the center of his mind the knowledge that "man's freedom to be happy, quite independently of his individual proclivities thereto, is exercised within a framework of political and economic freedom."

As for those "tremendous trifles" which can play so large a part in creating the feeling or, if you like, the illusion of happiness, my correspondent reminded me that "Our world provides us prodigious evidence that this evanescent happiness is a refinement enjoyed by a morally and materially well-fed civilization . . . a highly sophisticated *joie de vivre*." She expressed a not unreasonable doubt that Buchenwald "left time for contemplation of the incommunicable niceties, or whether, in the stifled air of a sealed railroad car, the elusive breath of those untranslatable ecstasies fluttered." In short, my correspondent would have had me remember that "Jefferson saw simply that beneath the esthetic man dwells the economic man."

Yet, however true it is that no man can be happy on a chronically empty stomach, and that prolonged hunger is the shortest road to barbarism, something of a case can be made for the contention that the capacity for the enjoyment of little things diminishes in direct ratio to the degree of material well-being of which we are in possession. The real sybarite rolls life on his tongue only for that brief period following deprivation when the small pleasures dulled by custom have been brought alive for him again. I did not learn how acute such pleasures could be, how immensely their savor could be sharpened, until,

at the age of twenty-one, I spent a summer as a member
of a survey crew in the woods of the Pacific Northwest.
My deprivations were less than minor compared with
those endured by any foot soldier in Korea, let us say, but
they served a similar function in pointing up the more
trifling satisfactions of life. For weeks my bed had been
the ground wherever we were camped, and because we
had to travel fast and travel light, it was without benefit
of sleeping bag or blanket, for which a night-fire was the
substitute. For a youngster who loved the woods and
fancied himself in a hard-bitten role, this was of course
not hardship, but fun. And when I returned to Seattle
at the end of summer I experienced a series of small
sensuous delights. Never before had I so keenly felt
"the cool kindliness of sheets" or taken such exquisite
pleasure in the comfortable depths of a chair. And so,
too, I never learned the full joy of privacy until I had
lived, in army barracks, a completely communal life.

My correspondent erred, I think, in conceiving of the
capacity for the enjoyment of little things as "a highly
sophisticated kind of *joie de vivre*." The pleasures of
which I have been speaking are not of the same stripe
as those exemplified by the enjoyment of what the self-
consciously ambitious gourmet likes condescendingly to
describe as a modestly ingratiating but unpretentious
little wine. The more deeply imbedded you are in the
lap of comfort, the harder it becomes to hold the capacity
of which I speak.

The Wonder of the World

It is hard, I know, harder perhaps than ever before in man's history, to keep alive in us today this energizing sense of "the wonder of the world." It is easier by far to wonder anew at the folly and stupidity of this race which seems so ready to throw away its splendid inheritance. Man, even though he may have shed the naïveté, ignorance, and arrogance that once permitted him the fancy of himself as at the center of the universe, has not yet taken sufficiently to heart the truth that the animals which he, who has so flatteringly dubbed his species *Homo sapiens*, refers to in such terms as "brute creation," have made, in many important respects, a better use than he of the world they share with him.

Yet keep that sense he must, if he is to add anything more to the glories which are his, if he is not to abdicate the position in creation to which he has lifted himself by his own bootstraps—this creature of incredible contradictions and divided soul. Not only must he keep it if he is to reach again the heights in art and literature which he once knew; he must keep it if he is to live at all. Were his sense of it strong enough today, the threat of his great weapons of self-destruction would lose half its potency.

I felt these things most keenly a few weeks ago, on a visit to New Mexico. There are other American cities as old or older than Santa Fe, but there, in its tourist-crowded plaza, where four flags have flown over the Palace of the Governors—Spain's, Mexico's, the Stars and Stripes, and briefly, for two weeks in 1862, the flag of the Confederacy, one feels the far past to be more pervasive, its presence more immediate. The reminders are everywhere and constant: in its ancient buildings, in the faces of its Indian and Spanish natives, in the long valley through which Coronado passed four centuries ago. And now, thirty miles to the northwest, as the crow flies, there stands in Los Alamos a cradle of the incalculable future.

In that proximity, there is, it seems to me, an arresting irony: that in this valley, where time has moved in such a slow stream, where so much has resisted its passage, there should have come into being this hatchery of science, holding within it the promise either of man's doom or his great betterment. About fifty miles northeast of the Los Alamos atomic plant lies the pueblo of Taos, where life has followed an almost identical pattern for centuries—for just how many we cannot be sure, but that communal life was already old when Coronado came.

The junction of past and present has always proved stimulating to writers. And the fact that the Southwest, particularly Arizona and New Mexico, makes one conscious of time—not in the clock sense, but in somewhat the same way it is felt when we live beside the tides of the sea—accounts in some measure, I think, for the attraction the region has held for the creative worker. Its wealth of material, its dramatic and colorful history, are only the outer wrappings of this attraction. Nor is it only because the Southwest deepens in us the sense of time, of the long perspective, that artists of one kind or another have found there food for the spirit. It is the kind of country that quickens man's curiosity about the important things, which carries his mind back to origins and causes, pricks him into speculation about the fundamentals of life and death.

It stimulates, too, his sense of wonder. Sophistication, which might almost be described as a numbing of the sense of wonder, always results eventually in a loss of depth, in a preoccupation, however cleverly expressed, with the surface of things; you can trace that development in the history of any literature. It is only natural that religion and art, stemming from the sense of wonder, should have played so great a part in the life of the Indians of this region. For that sense is fed in so many ways by the character of the physical environment: by the hugeness of the land itself, with the Grand Canyon at the apex; by the extreme violence of its climatic disturbances; by the blazing depths of its night skies. This is the kind of land that cradled the great religions of the world, and out of which came the great poetry of the Hebrew prophets and psalmists. It will be surprising, I think, if it does not in time yield a literature of greater depth, perhaps, than any we have had.

In such places as New Mexico (Los Alamos aside) or on the high plains of Wyoming, where I stayed a little later, one can more readily than elsewhere—much more readily than in New York, where one's skin opens so easily to the current irritants and infections of our world —turn a deaf ear to its summons to surrender to the assorted bugaboos of the fear-infested period in which we live. Sometimes it seems as if we were all engaged in a hysterical parlor game the object of which is to scare the daylights out of the assembled company.

Our favorite recreational reading deals in elaborately concocted means of murdering each other; the movies are still searching for the ultimate in violence that can be crowded into an hour and a half on the screen; the last thing you will find in the "comics" is a laugh; the picture magazines are apparently determined to probe the relation between the seeing eye and the unquiet stomach. No sooner have we made some sort of adjustment to the idea of living in the same world with a released monster in the form of atomic energy than we are bombarded with books telling us that even if we escape atomic and biological warfare, the human race is a gone goose, anyway unless it stops plundering its resources, and pronto.

The opinion poll—one of the smartest conjuring stunts the Devil has thought up since he started in business— tells what we think even before we have made up our minds. It is only one phase of one of our favorite sports —frightening one another with statistics, which are the most grotesque false-faces made in our time. If ever we take to worshiping brazen images, ours will be a monstrous neon numeral set up in Times Square and its country-wide equivalents. Not so long ago a statistician's handful of contented exhibitionists and confession-starved individuals submitted to detailed questioning on its sex habits, and the published results, now known to the world as the Kinsey Report, were received by the most gullible of all publics like a carved tablet from Sinai.

Yes, it is difficult for us to cultivate and foster the sense of wonder. Aside from our Pandora's box of fears there are, of course, other reasons why that sense has become so blunted in us. Chief among them, I suppose, is the fact that most of us, in this life which we so fondly think of as civilized, find so little time in which to think. For in spite of our annihilation of distance, we seem to find ourselves more hard-pressed for time than we were before we could cross the continent, or the Atlantic, in less than a day. One reason, I am sure, why international conferences get no further than they do is because harassed men jump up from cluttered desks in Washington or London and within a few hours confront a group of equally harassed men who have arrived as breathlessly from somewhere else.

Actually, of course, whenever we speak, whenever we sit down to eat, whenever we stop in at the corner drugstore to fill a prescription, there is occasion for wonder. The mystery of language, the shrouded early history of these counters of communication that we toss about so freely and so persistently debase, will probably never be cleared for us; our only approach to it is that of conjecture.

In spite of all the scholarly writing about it, we don't really know the steps by which men learned to communicate with one another, how agreement was reached on those symbols for objects and ideas which became the accepted words within the tribe.

And what could be greater cause for unending wonder than the elaboration of human diet and medicine? Its early history, too, hides in the dim past. That man, as a carnivorous animal, should have preyed on the flesh of other creatures, is no cause for wonder, but our minds, if we stop to think, must be teased by his daring experimentation in the use of other foods which we have come to accept as a matter of course. How did he learn that the bark of a certain tree could be the ingredient of a fatal poison; just how did he acquire his knowledge of the medicinal qualities of herbs? What an enormous, what an insatiable, curiosity lay back of all these extensions of his knowledge, and what a fascinating story it would be if it could be told in all its dramatic detail!

Van Wyck Brooks has made the observation that the enormous vitality of the nineteenth-century novel might be ascribed to the "excited wonder over human nature" which was characteristic of that period. For its teeming vitality was not a phenomenon peculiar to the literature of any one country; it was the century not only of Dickens and Thackeray, of Hardy and Trollope; it was the century also of Stendhal and Balzac and Hugo; of Dostoevsky and Tolstoy. It was Brooks's contention that today we have not the same wonder over human nature; that our age of psychology has not the same fascinated absorption in the spectacle of human conduct. This view is not as paradoxical as it seems at first sight; for it rests upon the premise that contemporary interest, as fostered by the new developments in psychological theory, has centered on the *causes* for human behavior rather than upon the effects of our conduct upon ourselves and others.

"Psychology," argued Brooks, "is one thing, and it is the dominant thing today. Perception and feeling are something else—have not the Germans proved it? It was they who invented psychology, and with the Austrians, psychoanalysis. But did they not lose two world wars largely because they knew nothing of human-nature? If they had understood the never-say-die disposition of the English and American mind, they would not have joined battle with it, so stupidly, twice. The Germans have proved how remote psychology is from perception and feeling—the qualities that have always been dominant in the great ages."

If we accept the validity of this distinction and admit that our interest has shifted in the field of human relations from the phenomena themselves to the causes, may we not then conclude this to be the reason why we are more often offered stereotypes by the contemporary writer of fiction instead of highly individualized characters? The scientific approach rests upon classification, and the psychologist likes to assign the varieties of human behavior to neat categories. More than a little of his attitude has crept into the serious novelist's handling of his characters; not only a tendency toward analysis rather than the exercise of perception and feeling, but an inclination to see the individual merely as a specimen of a certain kind.

Thus the weakening of our sense of wonder has worked to reduce the element of humanity in our fiction, as it has also eaten corrosively at the heart of poetry. In a less important field, might we not say that the decline of the familiar essay may be in part, at least, similarly explained? For the sense of wonder is, as I have already intimated, an essential part of the essayist's equipment. You will note its mark upon him, all the way down from Montaigne, through Addison and Steele and Lamb, to J. B. Priestley and E. B. White. We have become enamored with facts as facts, and collect them in our reading as a small boy collects postage stamps or butterflies; but for the novelist, the poet, or the essayist in whom the sense of wonder lives the facts are valued only for what they suggest.

After all, what is literature? The word itself is one of those that defy precise definition as we try to approach the essential nature of what the word stands for when we use it to designate a superior kind of writing. It is, too, one of those words that are variously applied; we speak of French, Italian, or American literature, meaning merely the body of writing that a particular country has produced; we speak of the literature of music, meaning merely the books that have been devoted to that particular art; we use it even to signify any kind of printed matter, whether it be advertising or railway folders. And, more specifically, in the sense which makes definition difficult, as what the Oxford Dictionary describes as "writings esteemed for beauty of form or emotional effect"; or, as still more baldly put by Webster, "that part of it which is notable for literary form or expression."

It is when we use the word to describe a kind of writing distinct from other writing that our definitions become incomplete or obscure. Certainly neither of the definitions offered by the two dictionaries I have cited can be regarded as wholly satisfactory. There are a great many books, surely, which we would unhesitatingly include among those superior pieces of writing we think of as literature in the special sense, but which we cannot esteem either for their form or their emotional effect. And "expression" itself is such a wide word that it must probably be admitted as essential to what we have in mind when we use the word literature in this superior sense.

No novel is so frequently spoken of as the world's greatest as Tolstoy's *War and Peace*, but can we say that we esteem it for its form—a quality in which, like so much of the world's great literature, it is notably lacking? And are there not books commonly accepted as literature— and in the classic sense—such as Izaak Walton's *The Compleat Angler*, so placid in their mood that we cannot associate them with the strong feeling implied by the phrase, "emotional effect"?

Just what do we mean when we describe one piece of writing as journalism, and another as literature? If you say simply that journalism is concerned with the immediate and literature with what is permanent, you promptly find yourself in trouble. For what our best judgment tells us may properly be regarded as literature, in that special sense in which we have been using the word, may so deal with the immediate as to give it permanent value. In other words, journalism may be literature, as were some of the best pieces which Ernie Pyle sent to his newspaper syndicate while he shared the ordeal of the infantry in Italy and the Pacific islands. Perhaps the distinction between literature and journalism was most clearly and concisely defined by Ezra Pound when he said that "literature is news that stays news."

But couldn't we say also that what makes literature is the quality of its observation? It is true that reporting, which is the basic function of journalism, rests upon observation, and that good reporting derives from the objectiveness, inclusiveness, and vividness with which the thing reported is observed. Then what is it that raises the quality of observation to the level of literature? Isn't it the faculty, which we associate with what we call genius, of being able to look at something as if it were being observed for the first time? Journalism can be hackneyed, and still be serviceable journalism, provided its subject

matter is fresh. But to be literature a piece of writing must have the quality of freshness in its observation, or its perception; it need not matter that the subject matter itself is stale.

The observation out of which literature is made may be directed either outward or inward and often it has both qualities; certainly that is true of the greatest literature. The artist receives what is seen into himself, and gives it out again. That is what Joseph Conrad had in mind when he wrote, concerning the aim of art, in his preface to *The Nigger of the Narcissus:*

"To arrest, for the space of a breath, the hands busy about the work of the earth, and compel men entranced by the sight of distant goals to glance for a moment at the surrounding vision of form and color, of sunshine and shadows; to make them pause for a look, for a sigh, for a smile—such is the aim, difficult and evanescent, and reserved only for a very few to achieve. But sometimes, by the deserving and the fortunate even that task is accomplished. And when it is accomplished—behold!— all the truth of life is there: a moment of vision, a sigh, a smile—and the return to an eternal rest."

And is it not because literature rests upon a deeper base than that provided by form, which can add greatly to our pleasure, and yet still is not central to what makes literature, that we need never take too seriously the despairing cries of those who tell us that the novel has come to the end of its tether, or that poetry is dead and will not rise again? There are, essentially, no new themes, either for the novelist or the poet; all the basic ones have been handled again and again. The manner of the handling has changed, and will continue to change. But literature, in the shape of those changing forms, will be made as long as men can see with freshness and truth, as long as they can keep alive within them the sense of the wonder of the world.

WORDS

Every word was once a poem.—Emerson

Words, as a subject for talk
or written comment, are almost on a par with the weather
in their universality of appeal. We all use them, poorly or
well, and for good or ill; even the least articulate among
us have some interest in them. They are one of the most
living things of man's creation; one might argue, indeed,
that they possess more vitality than anything else the race
has fashioned: what else is there that man has made
which leads an independent life? Words do; they gather
strength and lose it; they become blurred as do the eyes
of an old man, yet keeping in them something of life;
they gather evil about them, like some persons, or, like
others, prod our wits or lift our hearts. They pursue their
own ends with what sometimes seems a dogged intention,
and when they are utterly spent, and divorced from the
common tongue, not all the grammarians and lexicog-
raphers can put Humpty Dumpty together again.

We react to them as we do to living stimuli, but during

wars and immediately after them, words, particularly those that stand for big and ideal concepts, are likely to have a hollow sound and to have grown fuzzy and frayed at the edges, if not a little rotten at the heart. Except for the most simple and direct, they are not much good in time of war, though we are pelted with them to an even greater degree than in the intervals of peace. However much we may talk about them as weapons, when armies are on the march and the earth shakes, words assume a triviality which belies their true nature. They have a lot to do with making wars, but, save for those we have come to speak of as "cold," they have not much to do, I fear, with winning them. The best kind of words in war are like those of Field Marshal Montgomery: "I am never anxious when I fight my battles. If I am anxious, I don't fight them. I wait until I am ready." Or words like those of Marshal Foch: "They shall not pass," or of the submarine commander who quietly ordered, "Take her down," before the seas washed over him.

But if it is better to be sparing in their use when there is grim work to be done, it is well to be thinking about them and the power they have when the guns are silent. And not alone the power which they hold, but the delight which they can give. In what other medium of communication or, indeed, any other expression of man's creative spirit, are delicacy and strength, explosive force and soothing assurance so remarkably combined?

Words

Nothing, surely, is more alive than a word. They are man's purest creations, of a visible or audible kind. They depend not at all upon material aids, though they may use them, for their effectiveness, as do all other fruits of the human mind. Architecture, painting, sculpture, music, science—all demand a material intermediary of some sort; words alone are as disembodied as when man first drew them from his stream of thought. Nothing in man's progress from his bestial beginnings seems to me as fascinating, as teasing to the mind, as the process by which he developed these counters for his thought. All of us who use them as tools in our work must sometimes pause to ponder over their beginnings and to wonder over the frequently brilliant suggestiveness of the symbols chosen by those remote ancestors of ours who looked with fresh eyes upon the phenomena of nature and sought to find in speech sounds that would convey appropriately what they saw. How admirably and how often they succeeded! And I think that the coiners of Anglo-Saxon speech were uncommonly gifted in that respect, difficult though it is to compare the quality of a word in one's own language with that of another's, because of the long and intimate, deeply imbedded associations of the native word.

Yet, think of words like *dawn* and *dusk.* They are beautiful in themselves, and still, after long centuries of wide and continual use, untouched by time, as fresh as the day when they were minted. There is slowly spread-

ing light in the word *dawn,* both in the sound and the
look of it. And the soft and stealthy darkening that is
conveyed by *dusk* is not merely the mental reflex oc-
casioned by the sight or sound of the accustomed symbol.
As you look at it, as you hear it, you are aware of the
perfect appropriateness of the word. So, too, is *thunder*
one of the most evocative words in the language. And
though *donner* in German, *grom* in Russian, and *ton-
nerre* in French are good too, is not *thunder* the best of
the four? It seems to me to have more reverberation in
its sound than the others. Another excellent word of this
kind is the Russian *prostor,* for which there is no equiva-
lent in English, French, or German. It denotes a wide,
far-horizoned prospect, such as that offered by the Russian steppes or our own Great Plains. The absence of
such a word in English, so responsive to natural phenomena, seems strange, for its early makers, though they
did not know such great spaces inland, must already
have looked on the sea when their language was taking
form.

The Greeks, we say, "had a word for it." Indeed they
did, as evidenced by such fine creations as *thalassa,* for
the sea. Is it not reasonable to suppose that the word
was derived from the sound of water slapping against
rocks, or the side of a boat? How dead beside it seems
the Latin *mare,* coined by a people of far less imagination, much less originality. How few indeed—though
here, no doubt, I may encounter indignant protests—

are the Latin words woven into the texture of English which have fiber and life! They seem to have about them a synthetic, laboriously created quality which is absent from the words of Anglo-Saxon or of Greek origin.

We never tire of the words which man in his folly and stupidity cannot smirch and debase. Words like those I have mentioned and many others like them never grow drab or stale. It is, for the most part, the words which express mental concepts that we tire of, that we come to use with misgiving or distaste—the words that we have sullied or betrayed, words like *liberty* and *honor, freedom* and *democracy, faith* and *glory*. These are the words that need renewal and repair from time to time, and that need to be thought about as we use them.

Words are such sensitive things that even the way in which we spell them matters. I have always, for example, had a strong prejudice against the spelling *gray*. To my eyes, and I am sure to many others, the word *grey* is mistreated and misrepresented by the *a* spelling. *Gray* is not grey. Somehow, the letter *a* lets in light, so that a *gray* wall is definitely lighter in tone than a grey one. However intangible the reason, the effect is clear.

I have been thinking recently about those four-letter words so much talked about in our time, which, though still banned from the average drawing room, have been picked up from the gutter or hustled out of the privacy of bedrooms, to be openly displayed on the pages of our current fiction. I have been wondering if, in the normal processes of arriving at maturity, one does not learn to use them without shrinking or too great self-consciousness and then discard them? One reason for their re-emergence, I suspect, lies in the unsatisfactory and, in another fashion from theirs, the repellent character of the sanctioned words. These latter smell of the clinic, as the others may smell of the lavatory. It is strange, is it not, that there is no wholly satisfying word in English to stand for the act of sexual intercourse, one which neither degrades nor conceals its full nature, and one which can be used in no other sense? Just as all descriptions of the act, however rich the vocabulary from which they draw, must be either pornographic, scientific, or faintly ridiculous because the massing of words, however skillful, cannot catch its intangibility, so, too, the single word to stand as symbol, has escaped our creative power.

Perhaps, if the four-letter words had not become, whatever they were in origin, essentially obscene, they would never have engendered such powerful taboos against their use. May it not be there that a writer like D. H. Lawrence deceived himself into thinking that they might be rescued from their murky limbo and restored to the clean light of day? Those writers who continue to use them flauntingly have either not made the adjustment of which I spoke a moment ago, or else they employ them out of a misdirected resolution to be "realistic." They are insufficiently aware of the life, evil or good, that is seeded in words and which then dwindles or grows lusty and fat within the tissue of which they are composed.

Our greatly increased interest in semantics, the science of meanings, is not, I think, a merely chance interest. Certainly there has never been a time when the understanding and use of words was more important than today; never before, perhaps, so much. I doubt if there was ever a time when there was so much careless use of them, or a period in which they were so rapidly debased. Like money, they are counters of exchange, but with the difference that words are living tissue, sensitive organisms that require the most careful handling. When they are shoved in the slot like tokens on a bus, as if they were all stamped in the same mold, or when they are used, as they so often are in an age of universal and insistent propaganda, to act like the inky effluvia of the squid, they become obscuring and destructive forces of great potency.

Nothing more true was ever said about them than what Elihu Root declared in the course of his argument in the Atlantic Fisheries Case: "Words are like those insects that take their color from their surroundings. Half the misunderstanding in this world comes from the fact that the words that are spoken or written are conditioned in the mind that gives them forth by one set of thoughts and ideas, and they are conditioned in the mind of the hearer or reader by another set of thoughts and ideas, and even the simplest forms of expression are frequently quite open to mistake, unless the hearer or reader can get some idea of what were the conditions in the brain from which the words come." These remarks, incidentally, were made in 1910, many years before the word "semantics" began to be bandied about. And when we recover from our surprise that two sentences in a legal opinion could contain so much truth so clearly and so simply stated, we can begin to see in how many ways Mr. Root's observation can be effectively applied.

I suspect that one of the first steps necessary to getting ourselves and the world out of the mess that it is in, is to become clear in our minds as to just what we mean by certain words, and by what others, who use them in what seems to us a quite different sense, mean also. Of no word is this more true, of course, than "democracy," or, to choose an equally flagrant example, the word "liberal." I think the English critic George Orwell was right when he assumed that "the present political chaos is connected with the decay of language," and that some improvement can probably be brought about by starting at the verbal end.

It is not, of course, a matter confined to the loose or inappropriate use of words arising out of carelessness or ignorance. Mr. Orwell called attention to the fact that in our time a good part of political speech and writing is devoted, through a carefully disengenuous use of words, to "the defense of the indefensible." He had particular reference to the nice-nelliness with which some of the characteristic deviltries of our era are described. Thus the bombardment of defenseless villages has too often gone by the deceptively innocent term, "pacification." Or, when millions of peasants are robbed of their farms and sent trudging along the roads with no more than they can carry, such whitewashed phrases have been employed as "transfer of population" or "rectification of frontiers." When men are sent to prison without trial, shot, or bundled off to concentration camps, words like "elimination of unreliable elements" are called into use. In this fashion it is possible to name horrible things without creating mental pictures of them.

Orwell hazarded the guess that the German, Russian, and Italian languages all deteriorated during recent years as a result of the word jockeying that ensued as soon as dictatorship in one form or another fastened itself upon these peoples. That seems to be a reasonable assumption, because even in Great Britain and the United States, the growth of bureaucracy, if not comparable to that of the totalitarian states, has nevertheless been sufficient to make perceptible, and most unhappy, inroads on the language. Its influence has been in the direction of muddiness, clumsiness, and circumlocution, where it has not been definitely on the side of deception and concealment. We like to think of ours as a time in which plain speaking and writing are better appreciated than in some periods of the past; we are proud of the fact that Fourth of

July oratory no longer pleases and has lost its power to stir us; we boast of our readiness to call a spade a spade, but we are guilty of some strange contradictions of that attitude.

Language being the responsive medium that it is, deeply affected by the temper and attitudes of the period to which it belongs, it is only natural that the way in which words are used in our time should reflect our confusion and our awareness of shifting values—all the uncertainties and contradictions that characterize the period in which we live. But language is not only acted *upon*—it is an active force itself, capable of affecting our attitudes and ideas; and that is why we must give increasing thought to words and to the power which they contain within them.

Basically, I suppose, it was his consciousness of that power which caused Samuel Butler, in his *Notebooks*, to remark that "We want words to do more than they can." Every writer who is baffled, as every writer must be, from time to time, in his effort to communicate exactly the thought or the emotion he wishes to convey, sometimes feels the dissatisfaction referred to by Butler mount in him almost to despair. "We try to do with them," Butler continued, "what comes to very much like trying to mend a watch with a pick or to paint a miniature with a mop; we expect them to help us to grip and dissect that which in ultimate essence is as ungrippable as shadow. Nevertheless there they are; we have got to live with them, and the wise course is to treat them as we do our neighbors, and make the best and not the worst of them. But they are parvenu people as compared with thought and action. What we should read is not the words but the man whom we feel to be behind the words."

Poe was much too complacent, it seems to me, when he declared, "How very commonly we hear it remarked that such and such thoughts are beyond the compass of words. I do not believe that any thought, properly so called, is out of the reach of language. For my own part, I have never had a thought which I could not set down in words, with ever more distinctness than that with which I conceived it." That is an assertion with which very few writers, I think, no matter how large their vocabularies or how clear their thinking, would find it possible to agree. It makes no allowances for the intangible, for that shadow which projects beyond every provocative or evocative thought. For most of us, I think, know that there are some thoughts which are like chords of music that go on expanding after they have been sounded, or like the concentric circles that spread out when a pebble is thrown into a pool. The right word or words do what the pebble does; they do not build a wall around the thought; they project it.

That loving and perceptive connoisseur of words, Ivor Brown, whose "word anthologies" have afforded some of the most delightful of contemporary reading, recently

107

called attention to a peculiarity in the current use of words, so obvious that I am surprised never to have seen the fact mentioned before. Writing about "Words in Our Time" for the journal of the National Book League of London, Mr. Brown observed that one curious aspect of word usage today is the undeclared warfare between use of the long or of the short word. Two tendencies appear to be simultaneously at work. One, fathered by the bureaucrats (or was it the social scientists who began the wretched business?) makes for the increasingly pompous character of official language; the other, set in motion much longer ago by the newspaper headline, makes for shorter and shorter terms.

Both tendencies inevitably result in abuses, in absurdities, and the distortion of language, but I agree with Mr. Brown in his conviction that the heavier sin lies with the complicators rather than with the simplifiers. For one thing, the headline, with its breathless short-cut to communication, is sometimes imaginative or amusing; the language of the bureaucrats and the social scientists is never either. Like Mr. Brown, I would rather read that "experts are being rushed to slash costs" than be told that "the appropriate authorities are proceeding with all possible expedition to visit the organizational localities in order to explore all the avenues whereby a diminution of expenditure may be achieved."

Of course, one effect of language used in a perpetual state of hypertension, as the tabloids particularly employ it, is an eventual dulling of response. If a word is well adapted to headline use (which means, chiefly, that it expends few letters, though vividness is also a desirable quality) , it becomes so constantly employed that it begins to lose its initial value. "Thrill," for example; once the word carried with it connotations of shivers down the spine, but since it has only six letters, three of which may be described as half-letters, it has naturally been much overworked, and has lost much of its original impact. This impoverishment of meaning has had its direct reflection in the coinage of phrases used for promotion and advertising, and thus we find the movies, for example, resorting to "super-thrill." And "super" itself, as Mr. Brown pointed out, has become common slang merely because we are always killing words by overwork, and so "absolutely super" is an attempt to rejuvenate the tired word.

But enough of the iniquities of the verbal short-cut. They are as nothing compared with the assaults upon commendable English which have been emanating from Washington and London. The sort of mind that has successfully substituted "directive" for "order" is much more to be feared and even more reasonably to be attacked. The thing is so damned insidious. "Directive," for example, as properly used, means "a form of general orders outlining the features of the tactics for a proposed operation or series of operations" (Webster) . But it has come to be used as signifying any order at all, and it is, by sight and sound, twice as pompous as the shorter word. I don't believe Mr. Brown was writing with tongue in cheek when he suggested that this kind of bureaucratic blah-blah may have had its origin in the fear of being thought incompetent; could it not have been conceived in the hope that it would sound much more impressive to write about "units of nutritional intake" than baldly to use the word "food"? And fear of another kind—the fear of giving offense—might not that be at the bottom of the use of such a roundabout and insincere phrase as "underprivileged members of the lower income brackets" instead of the straightforward and concise word, "poor"? I call the phrase insincere because I agree with Mr. Brown that the current use of "underprivileged" is both disingenuous and absurd. "If," he remarks, "privilege is a wrong thing and ought not to exist in our society, then why complain that anybody lacks this vicious article? One might as well describe a sober man as being underintoxicated."

There is, however, one consoling factor in this conflict over the long and the short word, and that is that neither in our speech nor in our books are these two divergent tendencies as yet noticeably reflected. Nobody, so far as I am aware, talks in headlines, and nobody writes a novel that sounds as if it had been composed at a desk in a Federal bureau.

I have already referred to the chameleon-like character of words. It has nowhere, not even in politics, caused more confusion than in the field of literary criticism. Today, when words are used more carelessly than ever, one feels sometimes like demanding that the critic define precisely what, in his mind, is the meaning of a word like "realism." That particular term has a multitude of connotations. One of the most confusing things about its use is that it has come to be associated primarily with what is unpleasant, as if the unpleasant were any more real than its opposite!

Yet even if we use them carelessly, it is increasingly evident that we are becoming acutely aware of the tricks which the use of words plays upon us. It is true that the awareness is not altogether new; as Samuel Johnson long ago observed, "Among those who have endeavored to promote learning, and rectify judgment, it has long been customary to complain of the use of words which are often admitted to signify things so different that instead of assisting the understanding as vehicles of knowledge, they produce error, dissension and perplexity, because what is affirmed in one sense, is received in another."

One might suppose that the ever-widening channels of communication would work against the private interpretation of words, but that is not what has happened. As Holbrook Jackson remarked in *The Reading of Books,* "Even simple people who might seem to be inoculated by press and cinema against individual observation and deduction can put their own private construction upon words. The virus of propaganda has not yet succeeded

111

in immunizing the herd against an outbreak of personal understanding. No amount of education has entirely succeeded in doping the popular mind into complete uniformity, for however uniform the doped minds of the masses may appear to be, somewhere lurks the undefeated and non-gregarious ego waiting a chance of 'breaking through' and asserting itself. Often the last kick of indomitable individuality is against the accepted meaning of words; it is none the less a kick even if it misses its mark, like the legendary old lady who had always been under the impression that Cherubim and Seraphim were 'man and wife like Sodom and Gomorrah.' "

Not long ago, on a visit to the National Gallery in Washington, I was shown the museum's recent Egyptian acquisitions; among them was a small sculptured head, dated about 2500 B.C., so modern and so living in its execution that for a moment it made the world seem all of a piece. Or perhaps I should say I was reminded that actually it is. The sight of that act of creation, carrying its impact across forty-five centuries, has been linking in my mind with thoughts about the beginnings of communication between men. We have all come to take the first means of that communication—the spoken and then the written word—so much for granted that we incline to forget the supreme importance in man's history of his creation of language, and particularly, of a written language. Strangely, we are more apt to think first of his conquest of fire, or his invention of the wheel, or any one of the means by which he extended his mastery over the physical world, than we are of the greatest and most imaginative invention of them all—the one which forever separated him from the other animals. By one bound he entered the realm of free mind, by his creation of speech capable of reflecting abstract thought; by a second, in devising for that language a written form, he achieved the only unbreakable continuity in the world he has fashioned for himself.

We do not often stop to think how much has depended upon that second step. As Richard Albert Wilson pointed out in his fascinating book, *The Miraculous Birth of Language*, there have been races of people who developed a highly perfected oral language with a history of several hundred years, but who were never able to make the advance to a written form. "They were," he remarks, "forced by this barrier to remain in a vanishing present world, isolated even from the most significant achievements in their own past history, so that they could make no appreciable progress at all in what we call civilization. The Cree Indians, for example, who lived for untold generations upon the plains of western Canada, had no written language prior to 1841, yet their oral language was as highly developed in its grammar and syntax as the English or any other modern civilized language." It was a missionary who, in 1841, invented for them a simple system of syllabic writing of which they still make extensive use.

What a pity it is that we know so little about the evolution of language in its earliest stages! Our only knowledge dates from the time when men began to put down in writing the words which they were already using. It has been estimated that at least eighty thousand years have elapsed since true speech began, and what is known about the speech habits of mankind is confined to only about four thousand. Of the period between the time when man became articulate—from the first grunts, accompanied, as they doubtless were, by gestures, to the time of the first inscriptions, we know nothing whatever. All is conjecture.

But it is conjecture that is extraordinarily teasing to the mind, or more specifically, to the imagination. It is, of course, possible to draw certain deductions concerning the general character of this early speech. Frederick Bodmer, in *The Loom of Language,* has, for example, drawn up a classification of the elements of language appropriate to a primitive level of human communication. His guess is that they comprised "Substantives, or individual words used for distinct objects or events which can be indicated by pointing at things, i.e., such as our words *dog* or *thunder,* and at a later stage, for qualities of a group, such as *red* or *noisy*"; then a second group, composed of vocatives, "or short signals used to call forth some re-

sponse, such as our words *where? stop, run, come, pull!*
and names of individuals."

A third group would be made up of "demonstratives,
or gesture substitutes which direct the attention of the
listener to a particular point in the situation, i.e., *that,
here, behind, in front.*" Finally, there would be the in-
corporatives, "or recitative combinations of sound used
in ritual incantations without any recognition of separate
elements corresponding to what we should call *words.*"

Yet about the most interesting things concerning the
early development of language, we are completely in the
dark. It is easy enough to guess how certain words, such
as those suggested by specific sounds, came into being:
thunder, for example, which in the Old English original
closely approximated the modern form, or *hiss.* One can
imagine that when they were first used there was quick
and general agreement, and that adoption of that particular sound soon became common in the group where
it originated. But how agreement was reached when the
word's appropriateness was not so immediately evident, is
to me, at least, completely baffling.

How, for example, was such a common verb as *to
run* settled upon, and how was common consent obtained
for the use of the word *house* to signify dwelling? Were
there arguments, settled by the old man of the tribe, or
was it the accepted function of some inventive individual
to find words for things and acts, once the elaboration
of language had begun? Among all the many things we

shall never know, this is one about which curiosity will persist. Both in their performance and in their origin, words are indeed mysterious.

Sculpture, architecture, painting are all less perishable than the things for which most men live; but even they are subject to the ravages of time. They suffer, too, a further handicap, in that they are chained to that particular spot in space which they occupy at any given time, plus the added restriction arising from the fact that no copy can quite recover the indigenous quality of the original. And music, of course, addressing itself to the ear alone, has no power, as Professor Wilson reminds us, "of representing spatial objects that address themselves to the eye."

Small wonder, then, that Shakespeare, asking "Where, alack, shall Time's best jewel from Time's chest lie hid?" should reassure himself regarding a possibly permanent record of his love by answering, "unless this miracle have might, That in black ink my love shall still shine bright." For the camera comes, and the telephone, the radio and television, but the written word, the printed symbol, is the most powerful, the most far-reaching, the most capable of multiplication and renewal of them all.

Much water has gone under the bridge since sedate listings were the norm of publishers' advertising. We have to look sharp these days to make sure whether it is a brassière or a book we are being urged to buy. I for one sometimes grow quite bewildered when I turn an eye or an ear to the hucksters' crying of their literary wares, and I often wonder whether I have wandered into the wrong department. Here is a copy-writer who signals for my attention by asking: "Do you get up in the morning almost as tired as you were the night before? Do you often have to drag yourself through your day's work?" Just as my eye is prepared to find the name of a new patent medicine, it falls somewhere on the word "book," and I discover that I am being invited to buy a volume on how to relax.

Or, finding myself confronted by a line of large and bold-faced type reading, "What a woman!" and under it a half-page picture of an equally bold-faced damsel, I am about to look for the name of the theater where this new super-colossal drama is to open when I discover that this lady is expected to take her place as "one of the unforgettable women of fiction."

Such experiences have become so frequent as to be no longer novel, but the other day I saw an advertisement which made me realize that we are indeed on or over the threshold of momentous change. On the cover of *Publishers' Weekly* was a picture of a highly photogenic young woman, and under it the words, "Her novel is the book the entire trade has been waiting for." Nothing strange or new about that; her picture had appeared there before when *Forever Amber* was about to be published. My realization that I was standing on my head came when I turned the page.

There, on the double-spread announcing Miss Kathleen Winsor's new novel, the picture was repeated in smaller size, and under it were these significant words: "The recurrent theme of all our advertising will be this striking new photograph of the author." It was that word "theme" that shook me to my gizzard. The recurrent theme of all advertising would not be what Miss Winsor's novel was about, or even merely that this was the new work by the author of *Forever Amber*. It would be simply the pleasing contours of Miss Winsor's physiognomy.

Surely the handwriting on the wall is plain. The sober prophets who have been proclaiming that we were about to enter a new literary era were speaking more truly than they knew—but for very different reasons than those which they had offered. Here was in the making the literary revolution to end all literary revolutions. The whole basis of literary appreciation for the reader, all the sage advice that has been spoken or written about literary apprenticeship, are being swept relentlessly into the discard. Henceforth the bedeviled publisher need ask but one question of the aspiring author: "How well do you photograph?"—provided, of course, there is any visible reason for asking the question at all.

This impending upheaval must necessarily deal a death blow to the schools of creative writing that have been springing up all over the country. It should bring comfort and reassurance to those sour-visaged pessimists who protest from time to time, "But you can't teach anybody to write." And while the schools will go under, their loss should be the beauty parlors' gain.

There are, it seems to me, quite unexplored avenues along which this new development may take us. If you insist upon being logical about the significance of this revolution in book advertising, you must take the position that the use of the author's picture as a recurrent theme is merely a means of halting the wayward reader and causing him to read the accompanying text. Well, then, isn't there more than one way of skinning this particular cat? What's wrong with a publisher discovering an author with a face that would stop a clock, and using that as a recurrent theme? After all, pretty faces are a dime a dozen these days, and they have been displayed to the point of surfeit on the screen in all manner of advertising, and on the covers of innumerable magazines. Why not strike a fresh and startling note?

Rightly or wrongly, the craving for novelty is generally held to be one of the touchstones for the understanding of the American character. I am willing to wager an entire set of the Elsie Dinsmore books against a single copy of *Star Money* to prove that a face which is the ultimate in ugliness, if used as a recurrent theme, will halt more readers in their tracks than will the repetition of fare, however pleasant, for which our appetite has become a little jaded.

Whether that suggestion is adopted or not, it should be apparent to the least concerned reader that a new day is at hand. I shall have more to say in this chapter about other changes by which today's reader is confronted, but first I should like to turn for a bit to certain aspects of reading as a pleasure which seem somehow impervious to change.

A few days ago I had a letter from a friend who wrote that he had, of a Sunday morning, sitting before a fire of oak logs of his own cutting, been moved to pick out a book from a shelf of long-neglected volumes. It was Conrad's *Lord Jim*. My friend had read it first some twenty years before, but as he read again he thought, how much richer this book seems to me now, when I approach it again in the light of the accumulated life experience contributed by the years between. His experience is one that most of us have shared, and the causes for his heightened pleasure are so obvious that there is no need to say more. But I think that most of us—and this includes critics as well as non-professional readers— do not, in our reading attitudes, allow sufficiently for the part that mood can play in the measure of our enjoyment. So much depends upon our inner weather at the moment when we pick up a particular book—just as much as our reactions are affected when we meet a new acquaintance or renew the relationship with an old friend.

Temperament, Ellen Glasgow once remarked, "has more than reason to do with critical judgment." And so, she might well have added, have mood and the stage of our development as thinking and feeling beings. She went on to recall that Thoreau had said, in a phrase which Stevenson called the noblest and most useful he remembered to have read in any modern author, "It takes two to speak truth—one to speak it and one to hear it." In another sense, she asked, "is this not the way in which any living book must be read—any book, indeed, that contains the essence, or the extension, of a distinct identity? We find, in a certain measure, what we have to give, if not what we seek, both in the external world about us and in the more solitary life of the mind."

And even though the re-reading of a book may not result in such a marked change in one's reactions as my friend noted when he returned to *Lord Jim*, there is, I think, a quality of enjoyment peculiar to our return to those books which give us lasting pleasure; it is distinct from that which came from the first encounter. As a matter of fact, it is sometimes hard to determine which of the two experiences is the more rewarding. The first reading, to be sure, has elements of delight which necessarily are missing when we turn to that particular book another time; they are largely those of discovery.

The contrast is much like that we experience when we see for the first time a piece of country that somehow strikes a chord deep within us—something about the way in which the mountains look down upon a certain valley, or the lay of the land as we approach the sea. If we come to know well that particular corner of the earth, so well that it finally enters our innermost parts, we have, when we come back to it from time to time, a pleasure quite separate from that of our first glimpse—but with something added—the pleasure of recognition. And this pleasure is one that holds for books, too. On our first reading, if the book happens to be one in which there is a strong element of suspense, we have the first time a tingle of excitement which we are not likely to feel as keenly again unless our memories are very bad indeed. But that very eagerness with which we press on to see what happens has a double edge. It whets our appetite, to be sure, but it also builds up in us a kind of impatience, a compulsion to hurry forward, that makes us insensible of little things along the way. We miss a lot in our absorption regarding the outcome. And these are the things we find when we come back to the book another time.

Again, is it not the same experience we have in returning to that well-loved bit of countryside? For in addition to the pleasure of recognition—of the moment when we top the rise that reveals a contour we have carried in our minds from the first time we saw it, or the way in which a certain house folds into its background, there is also that occasional delight in discovery of the little things we have previously missed—the way in which a single tree is outlined against the sky, or how a certain stretch of river teases the eye to pass beyond its bend.

In the same way, when we return to a novel in which the delineation of character is subtle and profound, time and again we find ourselves aware of a touch here, another there, that we had missed at the first reading. So much depends upon that inner weather of ours. Any book that reaches down into life has no more to offer than what we bring to it, and what we bring is variable indeed. There are times when our response to life, and to the pictures of it contained in books, is so blunted, so tired or indifferent, that even the most arresting presentments of truth go unperceived. It is the same as with visual impressions. Who that loves painting has not walked through a picture gallery with eyes that saw color and form and composition, yet saw them without that inner response that at other times streams out to meet the visual impression? Many people love the slanting of sun through trees in that brief but magic hour before sundown, but how greatly varied is the intensity of delight with which it is seen! There are times when it evokes a similar magic in our thoughts; others, when we are scarcely stirred.

Why should it be any different with books? If they do not hold life within them, they are worthless as dependable companions, and we must give of ourselves to them as we give to our friends in life if the rewards of reading, like those of friendship, are to be fully enjoyed. It was Coleridge who divided readers into four classes: "1. Sponges, who absorb all they read and return it nearly in the same state, only a little dirtied. 2. Sandglasses, who retain nothing, and are content to get through a book for the sake of getting through the time. 3. Strain-bags, who retain merely the dregs of what they read. 4. Mogul diamonds, equally rare and valuable, who profit by what they read, and enable others to profit by it also."

In his description of the last classification Coleridge was not, I am sure, thinking of the practice of reading aloud, through which the pleasures of reading may be shared, though it was then, and for long afterward, a practice much more commonly followed than it is today. I was glad recently to note that Charles Laughton, who has made a fine art of the practice, has publicly regretted its passing. I know the practice is not yet extinct; not only do parents still read aloud to their children, in such time as can be snatched from radio and television programs; there are still, I discovered, more than a few husbands and wives who read to one another, beyond a bit from the paper, or the last *New Yorker.* A column I did on the subject brought testimony to that effect from coast to coast.

There were, I grant you, vehement objections also; the matter is one about which feelings are sensitive and intense. For the predominantly visual-minded reader—the person who is likely to remember that a certain passage is to be found on a left-hand page rather than on the right —being read to is often an act of self-sacrifice. And there is, unfortunately, a certain insensitive type of reader aloud—those enthusiasts who, without troubling to determine whether you are at all interested, insist upon invading your mental privacy at the least provocation— which should be erased from the population by some rapid, efficient, and painless form of extermination.

Nevertheless, there is a heightened pleasure possible for two—and sometimes more—congenially minded people when the reading aloud is done by common consent. This is possible, of course, only when there is a genuine sympathy of mind and feeling between the two participants, and for that reason an audience of one is likely to be the most successful. This heightening of pleasure is naturally induced more by certain qualities than by others. Humor is probably the chief of these; it gains enormously by being shared, as everyone knows to his sorrow who has gone alone to an amusing movie or play; and everybody knows how difficult it is to keep whatever strikes one as humorous or witty to oneself. Similarly, there is always increased pleasure in the reading aloud of a book dealing with experience of which two or more congenial people have common knowledge.

But beyond these obvious advantages, there is something to be said for reading aloud as a touchstone of literary taste. Nothing shows up a shoddy piece of work more quickly than to subject it to that test. It is a particularly effective check for the person who reads to himself rapidly; his eye, skipping along, will spare itself much that cannot be escaped when the act of reading aloud forces him to take each sentence in his stride. Nothing so quickly and so surely makes one aware of infelicities in style; the awkward construction, the inappropriate word, leaps out from the page sooner than it does when the eye is the receiver.

Poetry, of course, should always be read aloud, if only to oneself. The eye is unequal to all it has to give; for sound, there, can have equal weight with sense. It is difficult to appraise any poem justly except by audible rendering. But prose, too, if it be of the best, has its own subtle cadences, and while some practiced and sensitive readers are able to take these in visually, they are certain to be more apparent if they are properly read aloud.

It is difficult, though, to determine just what it is that makes some books lend themselves more readily to reading aloud than others. There are, of course, certain obvious exceptions; no book in which abstract thought takes a predominant place—no work of philosophy, save Plato's *Dialogues*, should be read in that manner. Indeed, any book over which it is necessary to pause frequently in order to come to grips with the author's thought can be dealt with satisfactorily only where the relationship is strictly one between writer and reader. And it goes without saying that any writer, whatever his content, who habitually uses three words where one would do, is for the nimble eye only.

Matters of style and content aside, perhaps the nearest approach to a general truth would be that those writers best lend themselves to reading aloud who easily establish contact between themselves and their readers. When you are conscious of this quality in a writer whom you have been reading to yourself, the chances are that he can be listened to without discomfort.

I have been talking about appeals to the eye and the ear. Books are capable of both, but what of those new mediums of communication about which the publishers are worried? How long, in a world increasingly dominated by comics, charts, the movies, radio, and television, can the book maintain its appeal? The picture, as against the word, looms ever larger and more omnipresent in our distracted world. Before long, numerals, except in our bankbooks and checkbooks, will have become unintelligible unless accompanied by or substituted for by those little drawings of the chart and graph makers—so many little men, so many buckets of coal, so many corn shocks. Not long ago I was looking at what was described as an applause chart—a graph designed to show how the Congress had reacted to the President's State of the Union message. It took me longer—and I am, I think, what the psychologists would describe as a visual-minded person— to follow the ups and downs of that reaction, as represented by the rise and dip of a heavy black line, than it would have done to read a few succinct sentences in which I was told at what points the Congress applauded most or least. Sometimes it would seem that man has swung full circle in this matter of recording his impressions; he began with picture writing on the walls of his caves and he is apparently determined to end with it.

Whatever we think of television in its present state of development, we can be sure that it will become a much more effective instrument than it is today. And children, even more than adults, are visual-minded. When the day comes in which there is a television set in every other American home, it is going to be harder still to inculcate the habit of reading. And even if you can, what of that satanic movement whose instigators are teaching the young to read ever faster and faster? The objective now, I believe, is so to train them that the eye can take an entire page at a glance. Suppose these busy agents of the devil succeed in producing a generation of page rifflers who are able to race through a library like so many locusts swarming over a wheat field? Reading becomes merely an automatic process for the acquisition of facts. What then becomes of its other values?

And what of the magazines and newspapers which absorb the greater part of our reading time—we who already read fewer books than any other comparably literary nation? More and more they are dominated by the picture rather than the word. The magazine that is read by more people than any other in the world's history is largely made up of condensation, being predicated, apparently on the proposition that the average reader is incapable of fastening his attention on any one topic for more than five minutes at a time. The weekly of largest circulation is one whose appeal rests primarily on the art of the camera; it has spawned a steadily growing number of imitators.

Yet, while it is true that the appeal of the book, both for children and adults, faces increasing and multiple competition in our distraction-seeking world, I believe that we do exaggerate the threat. For children, the book has the great advantage that, if they wish, they can turn to it again and again, as they often want to do. It is always accessible, in precisely the same form as before, as the movie or the television program are not. And we all know what a persistent habit, once formed, the habit of reading is. We know, too, from our experience in the Second World War with the extraordinary distribution and use of the Armed Service Editions, with what rapidity new book readers can be made (though we must grant the circumstances were here unusual) and how surprisingly wide can be the range of their reading.

Let us not forget, either, the strange mesmerism of print—that curious and so often spurious authority that seems automatically to invest a page of type. Every writer, I think, has at some time been conscious of the suddenly added weight his words assumed when they were transferred, either from handwriting or typewriting, to the printed page. We consider seriously words that wear the vestments conferred upon them by Caslon or Goudy, which, if spoken, we would disregard unless they were pronounced with the disarming persuasiveness of a Roosevelt or the passionate invective of a Hitler.

No, I think there will be readers tomorrow and tomorrow and tomorrow. There is something about a man alone with a book in the quiet of his room or the comfort of his bed which sets that experience apart from all other conveyances of information or all other exchanges of opinion or thought. For the speaker's voice or physical presence may come between the listener and his words; the motion picture flashes its images before those who watch it and is gone; but the communion between writer and reader can be resumed again and again. They face one another, author and reader, with all barriers down, and without the injected distraction of other presences. It is the most direct and untainted form of communication that man has yet devised, the closest approach to disembodied spirit—even more so than music, which must have its instruments—that he knows. He will not, unless he is an even greater fool than we know him to be, easily abandon it.

THE WRITER'S RESPONSIBILITY

None of us but is aware that
the end of World War II, unlike the first, left us without
a genuine uplift of spirit. There was relief, of course,
but there was nothing like the same spontaneous up-
rush of release, no comparable brightening, however illu-
sory, of the horizon. There were, of course, several reasons
for this: the knowledge that civilization had paid an even
more staggering price for its victory—a price so great,
the limits it might reach so undefined, that we could make
no true estimate of what that cost would be; there was
the realization that the problems of the peace were as
huge as those of the war itself—an apprehension which
succeeding events served only to intensify; and finally,
the liberation and use of atomic energy shook the very
foundations of our world.

Never, it was clear to us, had the human race stood
at such a significant crossroads; never had it needed so
desperately to summon all the intelligence, all the moral
force, all the courage of which it is capable. So long as

atomic energy remains an unpredictable part of human affairs, so long as the probability of its destructive force remains as great as its constructive potential, man's world must continue more unstable than he has ever known it. What, we found ourselves asking, will be the psychological effect upon all thinking and imaginative people, and particularly upon those of the generation which will create our post-war literature, of the enormous fact now lodged in every inquiring and speculative mind? Until we have bulwarked ourselves against irresponsible use of the destructive power now at man's command, we must all live under the great shadow cast by the latest triumph of his ingenuity. Every year, every month, week and day, every hour, it may be, that this new force remains an unpredictable agent, is a bit of borrowed time. Will it produce a generation of absolute fatalists, who will choose to live by the principle, eat, drink, and be merry, or will it create an iron determination to make the only bearable equation—one in which man's foresight, common sense, and morality at least equal his ingenuity and his technical skill?

These are even now, perhaps, idle and unanswerable questions. None but an arrogant and cocksure mentality would venture a definite prediction. But of one thing we may be sure: that what is written and read during this period of waiting will play a part in determination of the outcome. More than ever, it seems to me, a burden of responsibility lies upon the writers of the world. Literature, of all the arts, cannot fiddle when the atom is broken down and its unchartable possibilities for good or ill are released for such use as men may make of them. Writers as never before are faced by a set of obligations toward their readers. It is now more than ever important that their work should build toward the creation of reciprocal understanding and good will among mankind; that it should illuminate the possibilities and rewards that can be won from life. Man today is a scared rabbit and he needs reassurance and fortification of his faith in his destiny more than he needs anything else.

This is not to suggest that every novel written from this day forth, and every poem, every play, should append a moral. We know too well what happens to art when didactic purpose dominates the artist's work. But the content of our creative writing, it seems to me, must be constructive in purpose. Our writers, if they are to be of any help in saving man from self-destruction, cannot content themselves with pointing up the idiocy and degradation of which he is capable. If knowledge of that capacity is not now vivid in the mind of every human being who is not a cogenital idiot, it never will be. What our writers can and must do, if man's heritage on this planet is not to be lost forever, is to remind him of what he can and must be, if he is to survive as a species. To perform such a service will demand what John Dos Passos has described as "that firmly anchored ethical standard that American writing has been struggling toward for

half a century, that unshakable moral attitude toward
the world we live in and toward its temporary standards
that is the basic essential of any powerful work of the
imagination." And it means that the writer who cannot
find an affirmative base from which to portray the world
about him is wasting not only his time but our own.

This need holds for novelists and poets as much as
it does for writers of any other sort. Such an approach
demands no retreat from a realistic attitude; it requires
simply an honest effort toward balance in regarding the
complexities of the human being—the kind of balance
that was too often lacking in the facile cynicism that
fattened in our books during the period between the
Wars. Though some of it was honest and deeply induced,
too much of it was merely the product of a fashionable
attitude, the succumbing to a herd instinct.

It was a period in which too many writers, as Charles
Morgan has observed, made a deliberate refusal to choose,
maintain, and accept responsibility for a point of view.
"It was for this reason a deeply unhappy age, so bitterly
aware of its inadequacy that it sought wild compensa-
tions, organizing itself into groups or surrendering to the
'leader-principle,' as a lost and panic-stricken child will
hide its face in the skirt of any passer-by, only to look
up presently into the eyes of a forbidding stranger."

There never was a time, I think, in which the writer,
and particularly the young writer, faced as many chal-

lenges as he does today. Merely to live in this disordered world of ours, to carry on a day-to-day existence that makes sense and seems geared to some worthwhile purpose, is in itself a challenge to our sense of proportion, to our sense of perspective. How much more, then, is it so in the case of those who undertake to reflect and interpret this world we live in, those who feel they have something to say to us and who would like, if possible, to bring some illumination to the life we are living.

These challenges are of two kinds. There are the basic ones, which concern the writer as an individual, just as they concern all of us at this moment in the world's history, but which necessarily have their effect upon his work. In addition to these, there are the problems which are his specific concern as an artist—the problems that are peculiar to his craft at this particular moment.

In what I have called the basic group, he is confronted first of all by the predominant character of the time. Contemporary writers have defined it in phrases which, though varied, rest upon the same idea. They have called it the age of perplexity, the century of fear, the age of anxiety. That these are apt designations we are all aware. Men today are apprehensive to a degree which certainly has never been exceeded, if ever equaled. And so the first challenge to the writer, as to all of us, is to his courage, to his capacity for hope and determination.

There is another predominant aspect of our age which, while it affects us all, has a particular significance for the

writer. It is the submergence of the individual life. Never
before has the race been so acutely conscious of mankind
in the mass; never has our belief in the importance of
the individual been so sorely tried. And that is a condition which strikes at the core of the novelist's art and
threatens the life of poetry. As Storm Jameson observed
several years ago, the novelist today "sees that there are
moments in the history of the human race when what
is personal in man is less important than the fears and
hopes, the impulses he shares with a great many of his
fellows. He suspects that this is such a moment. And
perhaps he despairs. He thinks: If I am to write about
this movement, this change, it will dwarf any men and
women I can conceive. It will depersonalize them."

It is true, of course, that there are times when what
is personal in a man should or must be subordinated to a
welfare that is larger than his own; it is true not only for
masses of men in certain crises; it is true for every individual life, in whatever time it is lived. Yet the novelist
cannot lose sight of personal values, of individual desires
and problems. He cannot, if he is to be effective, write
abstractly. Our understanding of how men live, of what
life means to them, can be clarified and deepened only
by studying the individual relationships of one man, one
woman, to another, or that individual's relationship to
his family, his social group, his country, to humanity as a
whole, and to God. Out of these relationships issue conflicts and adjustments of various kinds, and it is in these

that the novelist finds his richest material. But to present these conflicts and adjustments effectively, he must individualize them. Thus we have another challenge to the writer imposed upon him by the character of his time; in this case a challenge to his ability to keep in balance his awareness of the tremendous currents which affect us all and his sense of the individual's importance.

There is still a third condition of our period with which the writer must deal both as an individual and as an artist. It is what the Swiss writer Picard has referred to as the disjointedness of our time. His thesis is that modern man, whose inner world is chaotic, is constantly facing an equally chaotic outer world, where momentary impressions are rained upon him in quick succession, without connection or order of any kind. As typical manifestations of this condition he instances the radio, with its interminable abrupt transitions, and the increasingly scattered character of our magazines, particularly those on the lower intelligence level, which seem to devote less and less space to more and more topics. The newsreel, which shuttles us back and forth between tragedy and comedy, horror and nonsense, in a matter of seconds, is perhaps an even more striking instance. And the modern interest in man's unconscious has served to intensify the disjointedness by which we are surrounded, for chaos reigns in the unconscious. Because so much of our world presents itself to us in this fragmentary fashion, like the unrelated objects in a surrealist painting, it becomes increasingly hard for us to see life steadily and see it whole.

These, then, are some of the conditions of our time which not only have a direct bearing on our lives as human beings, but create as well the atmosphere in which the writer must conceive and carry on his work. But he is subject also to various conditions peculiar to him in his role as artist, and some of these, too, offer challenges which he must meet. He has, for one thing, been living through a period of intense experimentation; all the arts have been in a ferment of change. Whenever such periods occur, as they must, if art is not to stagnate, there comes a time when the paramount need is not for continued experimentation, but for consolidation. The moment inevitably arrives when what has been gained by the experimenters must be fused with what is of permanent value in the traditional. And that moment, I suspect, is here.

In all revolutions, whether political or literary, there are inevitably excesses in the direction of change and an indiscriminate discarding of traditional values. It would be unreasonable to insist that nothing constructive had been accomplished by the revolution which T. S. Eliot and others wrought in poetry; also, it would be blindness to deny that some of the forces which they set in motion have been harmful to poetry, in their destructive effect upon abiding values. The same may be said of the influence which writers like James Joyce and Virginia Woolf exerted upon the art of fiction. They deepened our conception of the subjective method in the novel, but they also deflected us from concern with its narrative function.

It is essential to all living things, whether they are forms of art or forms of life, that there be an interplay, an exchange between the old and the new; that is one of the first axioms to be drawn from Nature. In that interesting book about the tribal life of the Kiowa Indians, *The Ten Grandmothers*, there is a passage which delighted me by its homely but vivid illustration of this ancient truth. Two Kiowa young men are talking. Eagle Plume's father has just died, and by tribal tradition his horse should be killed where he was buried. It happened that the Kiowas just then were going through a difficult time, and Eagle Plume's friend, Wood Fire, remonstrates. "This is a good horse," he says. "People will need good horses." But Eagle Plume replies, "This is what my father would want," and cuts the horse's throat. Afterward, as they sit talking, Wood Fire remarks, "That is the end of one kind of living. I think all the old things will be dead soon." They begin to argue about the unwillingness of some people to give the old things up, and the right of others to get new things started. Eagle Plume felt very old as he said to his friend, "You have to have new things. You have to have new springs to make the grass grow. But grass grows out of the old earth. You have to have old things for new things to have roots in. That's why some people have to keep old things going and some people have to push new things along. It's right for both of them. It's what they have to do."

There, reduced to its simplest terms, you have the age-old conflict between tradition and innovation. Eagle Plume, taking his analogy direct from Nature as an Indian would, is saying precisely the same thing that André Gide reports himself as once thinking: "It suddenly seemed clear to me that if there were no names in the history of art except those belonging to the creators of new forms there would be no culture; the very word implied a continuity, and therefore it called for disciples, imitators and followers to make a living chain: in other words, a tradition." Or, as John Buchan once put it: "[If a man regards the past] as the matrix of present and future, whose potency takes many forms but is not diminished, then he will cherish it scrupulously and labour to read its lessons, and shun the heady shortcuts which end only in blank walls. He will realize that in the cycle to which we belong we can see only a fraction of the curve, and that properly to appraise the curve and therefore to look ahead, we may have to look back a few centuries to its beginning."

In all departments of human activity there must be this shuttling, this backward and forward motion, this interplay of forces. So far as literature and the other arts are concerned, it is when we have absolute intolerance of the representatives of one force for the other that we get the dry rot of sterile repetition or the gross exaggerations, the absurd extremes by which the intolerant innovator proclaims his absolute freedom from tradition. There is no more absolute freedom in art than there is in human liberty. Our own time, being a period of violent experimentation in all fields of activity, has seen a great deal of condescension toward those who have worked with one eye on the curve of which John Buchan reminds us. It might make a profitable half hour to sit down and compile a list of those whom we think of as the acknowledged great in literature, in painting and music, and to find how many of them could not properly be classed as belonging among the innovators—at least not in the sense of those whose aim was to break completely from the curve of tradition.

The challenges to the writer that I have so far mentioned cannot be exaggerated. Their vitality is such that they must be met, if literature as we have known it is to survive at all. Most serious of all is the threat of the omnipotent state, but before I go on to that I should like to say a word or two about those other challenges which arise from the special conditions confronting the writer's craft today. They derive from the various assaults upon the writer's integrity which have been created by the growing commercializing influences to which the literary career has been subjected. These, I believe, can be, and are, exaggerated. I am not referring to the siren song of Hollywood alone. It is a time when literary opportunism is in the literary air. There are publishers who are the best friends that a writer could have in relation to his work; there are others who can be his worst enemies, those who urge him into production, after a first success, before he is ready. There are literary agents who are helpful in many ways besides the matter of marketing, and there are those with whom their commission is the paramount consideration. It is no easy matter these days for the young writer of a first success to keep his head; that requires an unusual sense of balance and proportion. One evening, during a discussion of what writers are thinking about today, I heard the publicity director of one of our large publishing houses, in a confessional mood, say that she regarded the job she performs as one of the heaviest handicaps against which the young writer has to contend. She had watched too many egos disastrously inflate as a result of the promotion that had been considered necessary. The writer today lives in a world of increasing ballyhoo, and heaven help him if he lacks a sense of humor about himself.

These are challenges that, though real, are wholly within the writer's control. To meet them demands no more than a sense of dedication to one's craft, and in the writer who is an artist that sense is almost identical with the instinct for self-preservation. If that sense is acute within him, he can take Hollywood in his stride; there are those who have done so. Let us not concern ourselves with those unfavorable conditions which every writer, if he has character enough, can handle for himself. The gravest danger for the future of creative writing is of another kind.

I have said elsewhere in this book that men will continue to create literature as long as they are able to see with freshness and truth. Now and then a hue and cry is raised about outworn literary forms; we are told that the novel is nearing its end, that poetry is finished, or soon will be. Neither, I think, is likely, but, in any case, the matter of forms, or their continuance, need not disturb us. Man will always continue to invent new forms, or renovate old ones, in order to express his feeling about the world he lives in, so long as he is free to do so. But today that freedom is endangered, and the artist is in mortal peril. Should totalitarian concepts conquer, literature as we have known it is doomed.

During the nineteenth century in Russia the novel, one of the most eloquent forms that man has devised to reflect his reaction to life, was carried to a point of truth and illumination never matched, before or since. This was accomplished under a form of government which we of the Western world think of as despotism. To a degree, it was, but in spite of its prohibitions it still retained respect for the individual human life. The plainest evidence of that difference may be found in the treatment accorded those who were found guilty of political offense. Many of the men who rule Russia today would not be alive had "the liquidation of undesirable elements" been then in effect.

Today the Russian novelist is as much a state slave as the engineer whose responsibility is factory production. He may see with freshness and truth, so far as he can without being permitted knowledge of the world outside the bounds of the Union of Soviet Socialist Republics. But he cannot write with freshness and truth and have his work published; he must write what the state demands. One of Russia's most popular writers, Fadayev, who is among the privileged few permitted to visit abroad, asserted recently at a literary gathering in London that all subjective writing was bad writing because it stressed the writer's own feelings. It was "egotistical and therefore worthless." Thereby, in one phrase, he had discarded the larger part of the world's great literature. The Russian writer, if he is to enjoy official favor, must give expression only to mass feelings, or, to put it more exactly, to those sentiments and convictions which the state approves.

It is ironic that the dreadful world in which we live today is in large part the net result of men's good intentions, the product of divergent and fiercely held ideas as to what body of ideas, adopted by all, will make all men happy. What is most frightening in our situation is that men have all but abandoned the art of persuasion. As the French writer, Albert Camus, puts it, "Mankind's long dialogue has just come to an end," and we face the realization that a man with whom one cannot reason is a man to be feared.

Fear grips modern man by the throat. The diehard Tory's implacable resistance to change and the flight to Communism of the worker and peasant stem from a common source. Each acts from a desire for security—a commodity that has no existence in nature, of which civilized man has forgotten that he is a part. You cannot expect a great literature from a people that is dominated by fear; you cannot expect anything that has nobility of spirit. What you get is a whine or a snarl or a whimper, the same as you get from a thoroughly frightened man who surrenders to his fright.

The ages of confidence are the great ages of literature, the great ages of art. Such was the Elizabethan age, when men's eyes swept the horizon with ardent hope; such, we are beginning reluctantly to grant, was the Victorian, in spite of its doubts—which are a different thing from fears. And such our own can be, if it can find a spiritual base from which to cope with its problems.

We have already had one literary generation which surrendered to its fears; it called itself the Lost Generation. Let us not have another. Because it had seen men make a mockery of love and faith and honor, it told itself that these were mirages forever beyond our reach. And what it wrote, it wrote with only one half of man's nature, and seeing only half. Some of this writing was good; as good as the writing of a man who is not a whole man can be. But it is not good enough for our time, as some of our young writers are beginning to perceive. The literature of the second half of the twentieth century, if there is to be a literature at all, will have to be a literature of courage.

Reporting is one of the great American skills. In that craft, we are acknowledged leaders, as much as we are in the technique of industrial production. It is a skill which we acquired early and have consistently developed. Reporting is the triumph of our journalism; for many years it has been, with rare exceptions, more dynamic than the writing of opinion on the things it describes. But what of its bearing on our literature? There is no doubt that its influence on the writing of American fiction, particularly during the past half-century, has been enormous. In some respects that influence has been salutary; in others I believe it has been deeply harmful.

It has been salutary because it has fostered the observant eye and has encouraged the use of first-hand material. It was an effective force in widening the range of that material, and the men who broke the chains of the Genteel Tradition in our fiction had, in the majority, been newspaper reporters before they turned to the novel.

It bred vitality because it maintained a direct relation to life as the reporter saw it. It was further effective, I think, in reducing pomposities and artificialities of style, as well as in curbing the sentimental approach. And there, I submit, its contributions end.

Reporting is, by its very nature, concerned with the externals of things, and that is why its influence on the writing of fiction has so heavy a debit side. It has given a surface character to much of our serious fiction, and has fallen short in value as a commentary on the life it undertook to describe. The reporter's gifts are a most valuable part of the novelist's equipment, but they are not sufficient in themselves to give meaning to the experience which the novelist describes. Such early realists as that highly skilled craftsman, Defoe, made up for the thinness of their approach to their material by a deliberate overlay of moralizing, plastering it on to a degree which today's reader finds it difficult to accept. But too many of our contemporary realists offer their readers nothing better, or as good, in its place.

Sean O'Faolain, the Irish short-story writer and novelist, once exclaimed bitterly over the persistence of the long shadow cast by Defoe on the writing of fiction. "One becomes so weary," he wrote, "of the photographic reality, that one wishes literature could learn again from Greek tragedy and dispense with character altogether. One wishes for that exaltation of mood in which the merely familiar drops away completely and the characters

achieve a certain timelessness that, like a piece of head-
less sculpture or a formal pious picture, holds one as a
symbol of the devout. For all differentiation drops away
at moments of high tragedy, and Hamlet and Laertes are
indistinguishable in the moments of their death. . . .
The greatest kind of literature is, surely, epic and folk-
song; and toward these two, literature, and in a way, all
art, is constantly striving backward out of the tangle of
its own sophistication to a dignity that depends largely
on the oneness of man."

This, I think, was an interesting and very suggestive
overstatement. The greatest novelists have known how to
use the photographic method to good purpose, but they
used a divining rod as well as a camera. And I doubt
very much whether Mr. O'Faolain would actually wish
to dispense with character altogether. Indistinguishable
as Hamlet and Laertes may have been in death, they certainly were not so in life.

But how deeply true it is that literature must constantly
strive back "out of the tangle of its own sophistication"!
That is especially its predicament now, and because sophistication draws away from the fundamentals of life,
what our novelists, with few exceptions, have been forgetting is that man is essentially a creature torn between
satisfaction and aspiration; in those two words, I think,
you have the basic and controlling urges in human nature;
it is seldom indeed that both are not to some extent
present in every man and woman. The proportions of

their mixture are, as we all become aware as life goes on, of an infinite variety. The saint is as free from the urge of satisfaction as any animate bundle of human appetites can ever be, though his freedom can never be absolute; and all but the most brutish or moronic of men contain within them impulses which rise above the satisfaction of physical or material needs.

Yet you would never guess the existence of this incontrovertible fact from the writings of many novelists who have in our time been hailed as realists, as honest and objective commentators on human life. They have chosen to ignore the reality of man's inner world, that complexity of human nature—which is at the same time so simple—that constant and universal struggle between satisfaction and aspiration which must be taken into account whether the novelist deals with its manifestations on a high or a low level of human intelligence and character.

This sense of man's duality is coming back into our fiction; because they have been widely read, I mention two recent instances: Grahame Greene's *The Heart of the Matter* and Alan Paton's *Cry the Beloved Country*. Since the last war that sense has been discernible in the work of some of the youngster writers. But I have found it more frequently in British than in American fiction, and I think we may with some profit examine the prevailing nature of our own war novels; the reflection of their experience in World War II was, naturally, the first theme to engage the attention of the post-war generation of writers. In this work the reporting capacity which I said had been so highly developed in our fiction is the characteristic by which one is first of all impressed in this new body of writing; it is in the more deeply probing function of fiction, provided by what I have called the sense of man's duality, that this writing has been weak.

Merely as reportage, undertaking to describe what combat is like, and how men behave under fire, these books have frequently achieved vividness and truth; they have unflinchingly set down all the filth, horror, boredom, terror, and misery which are an inescapable part of war. Where they have failed, and badly, is in the picture they have given of the American soldier as a human being. In the name of realism, too many of our young novelists have offered us, in their pictures of the American soldier, the kind of resemblance one finds in a cracked or beveled mirror. They have shown us, and asked us to accept as a credible cross-section of the American armies that fought round the globe, as fine a collection of prime s-o-b's, Kremlin fodder, and psychopaths as could ever be found under the light of a blue moon. In the book which had the greatest popular and critical success of any of the war novels—Norman Mailer's *The Naked and the Dead* —we were, furthermore, asked to accept as true a picture of the backgrounds out of which his characters came, so hand-picked and distorted as to match Moscow propaganda at its peak of misrepresentation.

Anger, says the old proverb, begins with folly and ends with repentance. Like most well-seasoned maxims, this one rests on a solid bottom of truth, but it is a bottom as narrow as it is solid. Anger can be rewarding, too. It was so in the case of an outburst of mine on this matter of our war fiction, because it gave me confirmation that the prevailing tenor of these novels was unacceptable to many men who fought in World War II.

In the column "Speaking of Books," in *The New York Times Book Review*, I had expressed sharp disagreement with a review of a British war novel, *From the City, From the Plough*. It was my contention that the reviewer, in summarily dismissing this book as so much sentimental hokum, was talking through his hat. What in his eyes had deprived Alexander Baron's novel of the right to serious consideration was, I pointed out, the fact that the men who made up the Fifth Battalion of the Wessex Regiment were, on the whole, a pretty decent lot of men, including even the officers. I added that the reviewer seemed nettled because no cases of battle psychosis were mentioned (the battalion happened to be made up of stolid country boys) and that he appeared incredulous because the unit contained only one deserter.

My own anger was matched by the letters which poured in from all parts of the country, and I was heartened particularly by the fact that so many of them came from men who had fought on the South Pacific islands, on the Normandy beachheads, and in the Italian hills.

American Realism

From an ex-corporal of Marines came this: "It was the most moving experience of my life to find that there was, in the vast majority of men I lived with for over three years—even among those with virtually no education or introspective sensitivity—a firmly entrenched sense of their own dignity as human beings, and a vital awareness of, and respect for, their fellows—two forces which grew into a firm affectionate rapport in the ensuing agonies of assault and garrison. Those cynical critics who cannot see these truths I pity deeply; they know not whereof they speak so glibly. And if they pontifically presume to imply—in the best Freudian tradition—that several men who risked death rescuing a companion did so because they are victims of unsatisfactory sexual relations with their wives or because of some polymorphous-perverse death-wish, they are mistaken. . . . To me, our highly touted war novels, notably Mailer's, in devoting themselves to a constricted reportage and a Freudian-mammalian conception of the infantryman, have received such frenzied acclaim because their literal descriptions have helped to provide our relatively uninvolved civilians with an easy sense of vicarious participation; and because their pessimistic portrait of the soldier has helped to absolve the American public from a half-sensed guilt due to this lack of involvement. The American war novel which will give the picture of man in totality, which will deal truly with, as you remark, the tolerance and affection with which men under the pressure of circumstances come to feel for each other, and which will treat honestly man's inherent goodness and selflessness of purpose, has yet to be published."

A colonel of engineers wrote: "It is time someone outside the army told the American citizen that his army either in peace or war is not predominantly composed of psychopaths, sexual perverts, drunks and prussianized officers, and that the only heroic characters are not naked and dead. After thirty-three years' service in the army, including regimental command in combat, I have yet to encounter any unit as rotten in morals and morale as those some novelists and reviewers conjure up in their imaginations."

The reviewer of *From the City, From the Plough* had jeered at its picture of the colonel who was killed leading his troops across a bridge, a flower in his buttonhole and a walking stick in his hand. This, he found, was romantic poppycock, and its use in the novel was evidence of its failure to tell the truth about war. Whereupon two Canadian war correspondents observed: "This morning we had coffee with a Canadian colonel who could have been the precise model for the fictitious colonel. Happily, he is alive, and he wears the Victoria Cross. . . . At Dieppe he led his men of the South Saskatchewan Regiment across a bridge under heavy fire, swinging his tin hat nonchalantly in his hand."

There would be little point in further quotations from the letters that came to me about our war fiction. Most

of them were written by men who had served on one or
another of the fronts, and their tenor was alike; on the
human side, the consensus was, these novels had drawn
a misleading picture; of the human being under the uniform, in large measure only the poorer part had been
shown. Yet the men who wrote the letters had endured
the same hell as the men who wrote the books; why the
discrepancy? The first answer that comes to mind is that
the novelists, when they sat down to write, had over their
shoulders the prevailing character of American realistic
writing of the immediate past; its strength was in its
rendering of visual impression, which is the better part
of our war novels; its weakness was on the side of human
sympathy and understanding, which has proved to be the
weakness also of our war fiction.

There have been exceptions, of course. Some of the
most humane writing about the war was the work of a
man who was not a novelist at all, and yet whose reporting, because of his deep sense of human identification
with the men whose foxholes he shared, managed to capture what most of the novelists did not; I refer, of course,
to Ernie Pyle. He never lost sight of the individual. Occasionally, in the novel, a writer like John Hersey duplicated his humanity, but in the main, I think, our war
fiction has warranted the reaction I have described.

Its myopic quality had its roots, I am convinced, in
the novels on which the literary taste of its writers had
been formed. I have come to the reluctant conclusion

that American realism, as it has been practiced in the novel, may fairly be described as the realism of a spoiled child. The distortion which has characterized our war fiction has extended also to many of our so-called realistic novels on whatever theme, to the end that they have for years past presented a misleading and very partial picture of American life. The vision of too many of our novelists has been restricted to seeing only what they have wanted to see. Popular fiction, of the type printed in our magazines of wide circulation, has worn rose-colored glasses; our "serious" novelists, on the other hand, have looked at their world through lenses that are dark and dirt-encrusted. A clear and balanced vision, admitting both the shadowed and the bright, has been all but absent from our fiction.

Because we have become a spoiled people, remote from and largely untouched by the realities which other great peoples, both in Europe and Asia, have known at first hand, we have become almost incapable of a true realism. We have been divorced from the broad and tragic base of human experience as shared by the whole people of a nation. While misery and fear, brutality and despair have multiplied in many lands, we have been subjected only to petty discomforts and deprivations. We fought our last war, and the one before it, with great energy and some small measure of self-sacrifice, it is true, but not with misery and horror shared with our troops, as it was shared by the peoples of other lands.

Even the Civil War, bloody and crucial though it was, left whole areas of our life untouched. Except for a few faltering moments, we have always lived in confidence and hope; the journey westward, in quest of fatter lands and freer life, has symbolized the national temper. Those trials of Job, which have been the part of every other great nation, and of which George Santayana said that until we had suffered them, it would not be known whether the Americans were at bottom a spiritual or a materially minded people, are still to come.

Our realism, for the most part, reminds me of the complaints of a healthy man annoyed by a passing and trivial illness. Because we have had so much, and so easily, it has grown increasingly hard for us to understand the pleasure and satisfaction that peoples less fortunately placed can have in the small recompenses of life. We are still children in the world, and spoiled children at that. How could we write realistic books? It is like asking a pampered child to tell you the meaning of life.

What then of the books that are being written in America now and which will be written in the immediate future? What may we hope for them to be like, in order that they may feed and foster that spirit of man whose flame now burns so fitfully and with so pale a light? For they have a part to play, let us not forget, in deciding whether or not man is to be discarded as nature's magnificent failure.

Let us hope that they will reaffirm, in a period whose

159

sensibilities have been badly blunted by mass murder and mass suicide, the inalienable sanctity and worth of the individual human life. Let us hope that they will tear off the ideological blinders that restrict the vision of too many young American novelists writing of their own time; that they will recover the truth that lay behind those too much mocked at words of William Dean Howells, when he said that the more smiling aspects of life were the more truly American ones (who can doubt it when he looks about him at the world today?); we may hope that they will rediscover the sense that American literature once had of the duality of man's nature, of its equal capacity for good and evil, and that they will build their books again around the core of that never-ending conflict. I hope too that they will come to know, if they do not already know them, those words of the greatest spokesman American youth has ever had—Ralph Waldo Emerson—"All life remains unwritten still."

One of my chief affections is for rivers. Nothing delights me more than to make the acquaintance of one new to me or to revisit one that I love and have not seen for a long time. A few days ago, in West Virginia, I traveled for the first time along the Kanawha; a tributary of the Ohio, its eastern banks were once traversed by the Warriors Path, coming down from Fort Pitt to Cumberland Gap, where the path turned north and was later paralleled by the Wilderness Road. Now those banks are lined at intervals by manufacturing plants out of which come, besides the smoke that drifts over the valley of the Kanawha, the basic materials from which the nation's nylon products are made.

Though its flow is curbed by damsites and its waters polluted by chemical refuse, the Kanawha, winding its way through heavily wooded hills that drop down to the water's edge, is still a noble stream, and one that stirs the historical imagination. For me its attraction in that respect was its association with the long and happy life of

Daniel Boone. I say happy life, though it was filled with as many sharp disappointments as make up the average lot, for if Boone had little luck in holding on to the lands he staked out for himself, if an ungrateful Kentucky caused him to end his days west of the state he had opened up to settlement, he nevertheless had the great satisfaction, denied to most men, of having done through all his life what he most wanted to do.

It was one of the most fully realized lives ever lived in modern times, and for that reason we cannot be sorry for him, no matter what ill fortune came his way. It was also one of the most incredible; he was the American Ulysses. My journey along the Kanawha, where he hunted and camped so often, caused me to turn again to the best book that has been written about him, the life that John Bakeless published several years ago. Like many great American figures, that of Daniel Boone was for too long obscured by the tangling of fact with legend. It was the great service of Mr. Bakeless's biography, by dint of painstaking research and sympathetic interest, to separate the two elements, and to give us an unsentimental but thoroughly appreciative account of one of the most significant American lives.

What a pity it is that so much industrious digging and so much colorful writing have been expended during recent years on the Western prototypes of twentieth-century gangsters—on the Billy the Kids and other trigger-happy figures who were not pint-size as men,

compared with Boone and Davy Crockett and Simon
Kenton. For generally speaking, the most celebrated "bad
men" were merely pathological killers and, one suspects,
often not essentially brave men. Boone had that lonely
courage that is the best of all, and the fullest self-reliance
that any man can attain. For all his close encounters, his
innumerable hairline escapes from death, he was never
a killer, save by necessity. Unlike most frontiersmen, he
not only understood the Indian as a foe, but as a human
being as well. According to Mr. Bakeless, he once told
his son Nathan that "in his whole life he was sure of having killed only one Indian and that was at the Blue Licks
battle. Sometimes he raised the score to three—never
any more."

But the story one prizes most, and the one that be-
speaks the esence of the man, is that told by the St. Louis
artist, Chester Harding (who made the only portrait
painted of Boone from life), of his visit to the cabin in
which, at the age of ninety, he found the old man cook-
ing a strip of venison, wound round his ramrod, for his
dinner. Harding asked him if, traveling the wilderness
as he had, without a compass, he had ever been lost.
"No," said Boone, "I can't say as ever I was lost, but
I was *bewildered* once for three days."

Though he was, as I have remarked, our own Ulysses,
and symbolizes to an extraordinary degree the best elements in the pioneer tradition, he has not been embodied
in our creative literature as fully and as suggestively as I

think, eventually, he will be. Had Elizabeth Madox Roberts lived a little longer, she would probably have completed the cycle of poems about him of which only three were published. She did, of course, make splendid use of him in that fine historical novel, *The Great Meadow*, in which, though he never appears, he moves, a presence in the background, as invisibly and as significantly as he moved through the forests which were his home.

Of all our folk heroes he is, it seems to me, the one in whom the stuff of epic poetry and of epic narrative is most abundantly present. He is all of a piece, and never out of character, and he is so completely, so unmixedly, our own. The story of American life is in one sense the story of American rivers, as Constance Lindsay Skinner so wisely perceived when she launched the Rivers of America Series; and like the Kanawha and the Ohio, the life of Daniel Boone has the flow of destiny and that mysterious beckoning toward what lies beyond, that is not only the appeal of rivers, but the essence of our American life that took its rise from them.

INDIAN SONG

On one of those crystalline August days when the intensely blue sky heralds the approach of autumn on the high western plains, I spent the morning riding and walking over the hills above the Little Big Horn, where "Glory-Hunter" Custer, with 225 officers and men of the Seventh Cavalry, fell before the encircling Sioux and Cheyennes on June 26, 1876. In this, the outstanding battle of our Indian wars, the enemy loss has been estimated at less than forty. Though the whites were vastly outnumbered in what has too long been misleadingly called the Custer massacre, it is also true that they were outgeneraled.

Insignificant though the Custer fight is in the world's history of armed conflict, no engagement, save the fighting in the pass at Thermopylae or the evacuation of Dunkerque, makes so strong an appeal to the imagination —none as much, perhaps, to an American. There was the last real stand of the race with whom we broke more pacts than have been made and broken even by Hitler and Stalin—and it was there that, though they won, they lost, irrevocably. Actually, they had lost long before, of course, but that was the greatest massing of Indian against white that had ever been attempted, and it was never again repeated on a similar scale.

From my guide, a young Crow veteran of the war in the Pacific (the battlefield lies within the boundaries of the present Crow reservation in Montana), I heard one explanation of the disaster which I have not seen recorded in any of the considerable literature on the subject. Though the story is probably apocryphal, I repeat it because Three Irons, now tribal policeman on the reservation, said it was told him by several old men of the Sioux. I prefer not to credit their story, because it diminishes the gallantry which we associate with the "last stand." The old men, Three Irons told me, insisted that Custer's troopers were roaring drunk.

Drunk or not, it was to prove the soberest day of their lives. All too soon they must have realized, when the overwhelmingly superior strength of the Indian forces dawned on them, that they would not see another sunrise. The story of their desperate effort to save themselves is written for the visitor to read, in the widely scattered stones that mark the places where they fell. Though there is one big cluster within the enclosure where their leader lies, the trail of attempted escape is plain, and sad to see. They died with prospects of great beauty stretching out before them, with the Big Horns and the Wolf Mountains ringing the horizon.

Like another field where a lost cause ebbed out in blood—Culloden, overlooking Moray Firth in northern Scotland, where the Duke of Cumberland, "the Butcher," slaughtered the clans under Prince Charlie, the Custer field looks much the same today as it must have appeared to the eyes of the men who died there, save for the gravestones, and below the gentle rise, in the broad valley, a few green squares on the farms of the Crows.

When will we learn to think of them—these Indians of the plains, of the desert pueblos and the Eastern lakes and forests—not merely as savages (whose savagery twentieth-century man has more than matched) but as the possessors, not only of the land from which we uprooted them, but of a way of life whose human dignity, spiritual strength, and awareness of beauty contained elements for which we may envy them?

I have recently been reading, with much interest, the Indian songs and stories collected by Natalie Curtis in *The Indians' Book*, a volume now unfortunately out of print. I hope it may some day be reissued, because of the particular light it throws on the character of Indian song, which, like that of any other people, does more to reveal essential temperament and character than perhaps anything else. As Theodore Roosevelt, who was then President, observed in a brief foreword to the book, "These songs cast a wholly new light on the depth and dignity

of Indian thought, the simple beauty and strange charm
—the charm of a vanished elder world—of Indian poetry."

It is not generally realized—due in part to the badly
distorted picture of the Indian which most of us drew
from our school reading—how very large a part was played
by song in Indian life. We had heard about the death
chant, and the song of exultation in victory, but we were
not told about the permeation of song through every
aspect of the Indian's everyday life. Most of his songs
were religious, but by no means all; there was, Miss Curtis
pointed out, "scarcely a task, light or grave, scarcely an
event, great or small, but had its fitting song." And while
in Genesis the creating word is *spoken*, in nearly every
Indian myth the creator *sings* things into life.

Because of its striking parallel with the Twenty-third
Psalm, I was particularly struck by a brief morning song,
one of the oldest Cheyenne melodies, which was cus-
tomarily sung by old men, often from the summit of a
hill at dawn:

> *He, our Father,*
> *He hath shown His mercy unto me.*
> *In peace I walk the straight road.*

THE LITTLE LAIRD OF
AUCHINLECK

The earliest London journal of the little Scot who no longer walks in Dr. Johnson's shadow has now been published. Like the rest of the Malahide and Fettercairn papers, those fabulous literary finds which Colonel Ralph Isham rescued for posterity, it establishes still more fully the claim of the author of the great life of Johnson to be regarded as an artist in his own right. And how delighted he would be, who thirsted so greedily for the world's approval, if he could know how far the pendulum has swung since Macaulay dismissed him as an obnoxious little snooper!

He proved himself supreme as a biographer, and now we see that he carried to what must seem its utmost limits the art of self-revelation. It is reasonable to say, I think, that from his journals, the greater part of which are still to be made available to the general reading public, we know Boswell more fully, more nakedly revealed, than we know any other human being who ever lived. His was one of the most complex of personalities, compounded of contradictions, torn even more than the rest of us by warring impulses. Yet always he saw himself clearly, without illusions, and could face and speak the bitter truth about the person of whom it is hardest to do these things—oneself.

No man, remarked Somerset Maugham in his own excellent self-portrait, *The Summing Up*, can tell the whole truth about himself. I wonder if he would not now make an exception of the laird of Auchinleck, for it seems unlikely that anything important could be added to the picture he has left of himself, either as a young man or an old one. Maugham thought complete self-revelation impossible both because of vanity and disappointment with oneself; if self-esteem sometimes distorts the picture, so too does our surprise that we can do something which seems to us abnormal. But Boswell, an exceedingly vain man, could regard himself with complete objectivity. He seems sometimes to be standing aside and observing another person. He took note of all his qualities, good and bad, and each seemed as important to him as the other.

Thus he far surpasses Rousseau in the frankness and balance of his self-knowledge. Mr. Maugham noted that while Rousseau told things about himself that seemed to him dreadful, he omitted many others, "virtuous or at least neutral," because they seemed too ordinary to be worth recording. But Boswell profited by the advice given him by Dr. Johnson, that great fountainhead of common sense, who told him, when urging Boswell to keep a journal, that "there is nothing too little for so little a creature as man."

How wide is the range between the absolute candor of Boswell and the iron reticence with which some writers have spoken of themselves! We had to wait two thousand years for Thornton Wilder, in his *The Ides of March*, to supply us with a reasonable re-creation of the kind of thoughts Julius Caesar may have had about himself. The factual jottings that Samuel Pepys set down in his diary, for all their occasional intimate glimpses of that gentleman in his lighter moments, never admit us, as Boswell does, to the inner workings of his mind, his heart, and his conscience.

In some respects poor Amiel, who was at times in a panic at the thought of embracing life, bares his soul as completely as Boswell, but we do not get the same effect, perhaps because Amiel wrote almost entirely of his inner life, as tortured, in a different way, as Boswell's; but we do not see him, as we see Bozzy, moving energetically and with that enormous gusto, about his outer world.

We speak of *The Education of Henry Adams* as a revealing autobiography, and so, up to a point, it is; it is revealing of a particular intellectual's ideological prejudices and his awareness, again up to a point, of his conditioning. When we have finished it, we know a great deal about the mind of Henry Adams, how it worked, and how it came to work as it did, but much of his personality remains as submerged as the greater part of an iceberg. Boswell may not have had a mind of comparable grasp, but it was by no means insignificant, and what there was of it we know, together with everything else about him. And as the whole picture of the preposterous and amazing little man emerges, we can see that with all his faults, with all his sometimes outrageous conduct, he was loved and his presence welcomed by many people, among them some of the greatest figures of his time.

There's no use wishing that all the good autobiographies and journals were as many-faceted as his. We shall continue to value them for what they give: Franklin's and Gibbon's and Rousseau's; Pepys' and Amiel's; Buchan's, Yeats's, Santayana's, and Sir Osbert Sitwell's. One does, however, have certain sharp regrets. What would we not give for a less reticent autobiography than Kipling's, called as it was, with his customary accurate word-sense, *Something of Myself?* Or for a Boswellian handling of Mr. Churchill's later years, not to mention those of his foremost collaborator? Or Shaw's, with his guard down and his mockery muted?

The flight of gulls is, I sup-
pose, one of the most beautiful things in nature. Their
downward, planing sweep is absolute perfection of motion—a movement and, at the same time, a suspension
of movement, of which the eye never tires. It satisfies
something deep in us, stirs us in a way we cannot define;
it is a thing utterly beyond our capacities, but to which
our response is immediate and complete. The flight of
planes, it is true, provokes our admiration; there is a bit
of pride there, too, for they were built by us, who have
not ourselves the gulls' mastery. But it is not the same
thing; we admire the power and certainty of the plane
as it sweeps across the sky, but we are not moved in the
same way. The gull's flight holds a mysterious element
which is poetry.

Watching the gulls as I walked along the East River
Drive the other day, I thought it fortunate that New
York, from which so much of nature has been thrust out,
at least affords such easy opportunity of enjoying the

simple but deep pleasure I have been describing. And as I thought about this the flight of the gulls began to stand in my mind as symbolic of some of the lacks that have been so often evident in our contemporary poetry.

In looking at the gulls there is a kind of release—and I prefer that word to escape—from the world that is of our own making; from the man-made problems, the self-centered perplexities that make up so much of our lives, and press upon us in a far more unrelieved way in the city than they do when, in the country, we are in closer touch with the natural world of which we are a part. Man is constantly needing to be reminded of the rest of animate nature and the earth from which he in common came. Smile if you like, but something deep in him is answered when he watches the cows slowly crossing the field, coming in from pasture, imperturbable and, if you insist, dumb. A little of his fretfulness, at least, slips away. As when he watches the gulls in flight, he is, however slightly, refreshed.

Now what has this to do with the lacks in contemporary poetry? It seems to me that too many poets in recent years have been trying doggedly to live completely in the world of man's own making. They have tried to build their poetry entirely out of the stuff of their own minds, out of that self-centered world by which man is increasingly hemmed in, the more so as lives in great agglutinations of himself. There had been a natural revolt among impatient spirits against "nature poetry." It had become mere prettiness, and the world of nature was too often reflected in the same conventional reflexes which had been repeated a thousand times over, until the pattern of these responses had worn grievously thin. And the young poets, reacting against this enervation, thumbed their noses at nature. They looked askance, not only at the word "beauty," but ceased to look for its manifestations. Come, they said, we will take refuge in our minds; we will build our poems out of logic and reasoned perception of this life that men live among themselves. And so they cerebrated and cerebrated, and stewed in their own juice.

It cannot be too often repeated, I think, that, as A. E. Housman put it, "poetry is not the thing said but a way of saying it," nor that the intellect is not to be trusted where poetry is concerned, either in its creation or its recognition. Poetry in its essence is felt, not apprehended, and something of what we feel when we watch the gulls' flight, or the cows in their calm procession, must enter both into its making and its reception.